The Clouds Are Big With Mercy

By Alicia Adams

Copyright © 2020 by Alicia Adams.

ISBN-978-1-6485-8785-6

All rights reserved. No part of this book may be reproduced or transmitted in any form or by any means, electronic or mechanical, including photocopying, recording, or by any information storage and retrieval system, without permission in writing from the copyright owner.

The views expressed in this work are solely those of the author and do not necessarily reflect the views of the publisher, and the publisher hereby disclaims any responsibility for them.

Matchstick Literary
1-888-306-8885
orders@matchliterary.com

Foreword

Alicia Adams has written in such a way as to scratch people where they itch. Her book is reality based because it springs from her own life experience. Alicia is a gifted writer and she has done her homework. What she has learned about herself and her family of origin, in counseling, she studied further. This enabled her to identify, with accuracy, the standard diagnostic categories appropriate to her experience. Her book is more practical than technical but technical enough to verify her assumptions. This book will prove practically helpful to anyone who struggles with O.C.D. with its associated symptoms as well to those in a relationship with people of this diagnosis.

Ye fearful saints, fresh courage take;
The clouds ye so much dread
Are big with mercy and shall break
In blessings on your head.

"God Moves in a Mysterious Way" by William Cowper,
an 18th-century hymnwriter who suffered from a
mental illness that included OCD-like symptoms

"One thing I would not let slip, I took notice that now poor Christian was so confounded that he did not know his own voice, and thus I perceived it: just when he was come over against the mouth of the burning pit, one of the wicked ones got behind him and stepped up softly to him, and whisperingly suggested many grievous blasphemies to him which he verily thought had proceeded from his own mind. This put Christian more to it than anything he had met with before; yet, could he have helped it, he would not have done it; but he had not the discretion neither to stop his ears, nor to know from whence those blasphemies came.

"When Christian had traveled in this disconsolate condition some considerable time, he thought he heard the voice of the man, as going before him, saying, 'Though I walk through the Valley of the Shadow of Death, I will fear none ill, for thou art with me.'"

- *Pilgrim's Progress* by John Bunyan

To the One who was with me
In my Valley of the Shadow of Death
And to those who still walk
In this Valley of Deepest Darkness:
May you find that even the most Ominous clouds
Are truly Big with Mercy.

Preface

Alicia Adams was fourteen years old when the first indications appeared. She was praying one night when a strange thing happened – a thought that was not her own slammed into her consciousness like a brick hitting her on the head. The content of the thought might have been anything from an irrational fear of being touched to a dread of microorganisms to an accusation of murder. In Alicia's case, the thought took the form of an attack on her faith… an attack so oddly timed that her eyes shot open in surprise and her heart began to pound.

She knew instantly that something very strange was happening. The thought had not come from her. It was unrelated to anything else in her consciousness. No chain of reasoning had led up to it. She had been intent on her prayer until the thought came… from where?

Alicia had heard of Christians being "under satanic attack," although the phrase carried no definite meaning beyond vague impressions of spookiness and unseen voices. She'd heard no voice, but in a way that only made it scarier. "It" had somehow got *inside* her head. Panic filled her, and for a moment she wanted nothing more than to run like a little girl, to Mommy and Daddy.

But she feared that they would only laugh at her. She was too big to run to her parents whenever anything scared her, and so young that no one would believe the devil was particularly interested in her. Her sensitive spirit flinched at the possibility of ridicule, especially ridicule of such an alarming possibility as that of satanic attack. Her father, she reflected, would almost certainly make her fears the subject of his jokes for months. It was much better, much safer, to breathe deeply, and then to try to pray again. Maybe then she would be able to sleep.

Chapter One: Into the Darkness

A month had gone by, and the peculiar experience had been repeated. At first it was rare, but the thoughts were becoming increasingly more frequent. They were stronger too, harder to shake off. Prayer didn't seem to help. She had tried to argue against the thoughts using such apologetics as a 14-year-old would know, and found it just drew her in further into the darkness. The thoughts did not respond to logic. She could argue against them, but they would simply go on. Alicia's resistance was being worn down by their sheer repetitiveness.

She was beginning to wonder if this was how people "lost their faith," another alarming, half-understood phrase. Maybe it wasn't a matter of being influenced by the wrong people, as she had vaguely concluded; maybe faith really was just "lost." Or maybe it was stolen! She still had the uncanny sense of something outside herself, tearing her away from all she thought was certain.

Just a few months ago, Christianity had been a comfort to her. She loved going to the small house church her father helped lead. She was proud that she could understand his complicated teachings and knew so much more theology than any of those other ignorant kids in her eighth grade class. Dad had said that there was no fear of God in them, and of course he was right. Alicia thought her dad was the smartest person in the world and that everything he taught must be exactly right. She knew that most of the people who said they were Christians really weren't because they didn't believe the right things, but she was confident that SHE had the truth. Her father had taught her well, and she felt secure in their little world.

There was comfort in that, even though just about everything else in her life was horrible. Her first few months of public high school had been a miserable experience. Alicia loved to read and learn, but she didn't want to be around the other kids. At all. She hadn't minded those at the small private elementary school she'd attended the year before. Her dad had said she must have the patience of Job to put up with their noise, but by the end of the year she was actually starting to enjoy them, although she would still have preferred home schooling. After all, what was the point of having to put up with kids' foolishness when she would never be able to have real friends?

Alicia still had never told anybody about her sixth grade teacher's charming idea. No one must ever know about that! Miss Gardiner had been concerned about the quiet, bookish child who was always avoiding the other girls. Miss Gardiner was very concerned about the social development of all her students. This isolation would never do. Alicia must be forced to have friends.

Miss Gardiner prided herself on action. She bought a book of MacDonald's coupons and began rewarding those who would talk to Alicia. First, of course, she made sure Alicia knew that her "shyness" was not approved of and that Miss Gardiner expected her to return any advances made toward her. Feeling intimidated, Alicia went along with it so she could escape the invasion of her critical teacher. She chattered and laughed and did just as she was expected to do. Then she had to stand by and watch her "friend" be compensated for the trouble of spending time with her. Miss Gardiner considered her intervention to be a brilliant success. She never knew that Alicia cried herself to sleep at night, convinced that something must be horribly wrong with her if her friends had to be paid to like her. What had she done that had been so bad?

That was more than two years ago now, and Alicia had long since stopped crying at night. Her parents had taken her out of that school at the end of the year – not because they knew what had happened, but for reasons of their own. They'd tried home-schooling for a year, grown dissatisfied with it, and then enrolled Alicia in another school for eighth grade. By the end of the year, she'd actually begun to believe that some of the kids in her new school really did like her! Not that that mattered… oh no. Alicia didn't need friends. If other kids didn't like her… well, she didn't like them either! She knew that her dad had been unpopular all his life too. Superior people like them were always rejected by lesser minds. And it didn't matter. Not in the least. It didn't hurt at all.

Alicia could deal with having no friends. But her newest school was more than she could take. To Alicia, any change meant there could be a new threat to her, and this situation was very threatening. A huge building where she might get lost, enormous crowds that pushed and shoved to get to their next class, deafening noise, foul language such as she had never heard before, shocking disrespect to teachers – not to mention the taunts and insults that came her way! She felt defiled just having to sit in the company of such awful people. How could her parents send her there? Didn't they care?

Efforts to talk about the problem failed. Alicia did not really expect her mother to take her feelings seriously, but tried very hard to present the situation objectively. "The kids are mean, Mom! Perhaps some of it's my fault because I read into it, but…"

"Yes, you do!" interrupted her mother. "If someone's smiling at you, you think they're laughing at you!" Mrs. Adams was correct in her observation, but was unaware of the reason for Alicia's paranoia. She still had never been told about the experience two years earlier.

"You always blame me," wailed Alicia, totally defeated. It must be true, she reasoned. It must really be her own fault. There must be something about her that was so awful that she would never, never have any friends.

At least she would get a break for Christmas. The family was traveling to visit their relatives in California. For nearly two weeks, she wouldn't have to be afraid of any mean kids. Now if only these thoughts would stop…

But the thoughts did not stop. They seemed to grow worse with every hour the Adams family spent away from home. Normally Alicia enjoyed travel, but not now. She felt so lost away from the security of her own familiar room. All the strange sights and sounds were coming to her through a mental fog. Her uncle's house seemed as menacing as the setting of a nightmare. But there was no way to wake up… and increasingly, she could not even escape into sleep. The thoughts would go on when she was worn out.

Alicia had not wanted to tell her parents anything, certainly not during their vacation, but there seemed to be no other recourse. The thoughts might conquer her otherwise and steal her faith, perhaps her sanity as well. But what could she actually say? How could she explain what the thoughts were really like?

She had never known there could be anything like this – the remorseless way they kept coming without her consent, without any reasoning behind them, and without connection to anything. She felt ashamed, as much of the nature of the thoughts as their content. She was sure her logical father never had anything like this happen to him; if he had ever had thoughts like hers they would have a logical reason behind them. She was really trying to think of some kind of reasonable explanation for her own thoughts; she came up with several possible reasons why a kid like her might have "doubts," but she knew that not one of them was the real reason why she was having these thoughts. She didn't know what the real reason was, but she felt that it had to be something else.

She hated not knowing. And she hated feeling so out of control – of her own mind! That was the one area of her life that she had assumed she always would be able to control. She might not have any say over whether she went to school or what happened there, but she could always escape into her own private world. Now that was becoming more of a nightmare than her real life. Something would have to be done.

With great trepidation she approached her father, who was reading alone. Her mother had already gone to bed.

Mr. Adams looked up from his book at his young daughter. She spoke without preamble, "Dad, did you ever doubt that God is real?"

Doubt was the only label Alicia could come with for her thoughts. She was only later (much later) to realize how inadequate and misleading it was. *Doubt*, for what seemed more like the attacks of the devil?

"No," said Mr. Adams, displaying neither surprise nor concern. "I have had doubts about whether I was a Christian, though."

"I have doubts," Alicia confessed, sitting beside her father and beginning to feel a little bit better. If he took it so calmly, maybe it wasn't really as bad as it seemed.

She felt better still as long as she remained with her father in the brightly lit room. He talked with her about his own struggles and shared a verse about how Christ intercedes for us in heaven. Alicia had never thought before of Christ praying for her and was delighted with the idea. And the child in her felt both important to be sitting up late at night and talking to her father, and reassured that now that Daddy knew about it, he would surely be able to make those thoughts go away. He would know how!

Mr. Adams didn't think of asking Alicia when her "doubts" had begun. Nor did he try and understand what was behind them. Even if he had, he might not have realized that Alicia's "doubts" were very different from normal adolescent questioning. After all, no one expects a child to develop a mental disorder.

Alicia Adams is suffering from a surprisingly common mental disorder. Along with over 2% of the population, she has obsessive-compulsive disorder, or OCD. People who suffer from obsessive-compulsive disorder often experience intrusive thoughts — persistent, repetitive ideas, impulses, or images. They are called intrusive because they are not created or summoned by the thinker. They are definitely unwelcome guests.

Intrusive thoughts may be woven out of whatever material the person's mind provides — often something that already has some degree of emotional conflict or uneasiness associated with it. Some people, like Alicia, have intrusive thoughts about religious beliefs. A new mother may experience intrusive thoughts about possible harm to her baby. Another person may have intrusive thoughts about sex. Still others have intrusive thoughts related to their fears of germs, of fire, of being robbed, or of accidentally harming someone. It is normal to have some anxieties about any of those things. Most people do. During an occurrence of full-blown OCD, normal uneasy feelings become exaggerated to the point where the individual becomes mentally ill, unable to function normally and consumed with irrational fears.

What causes such episodes? OCD is an interaction disorder, involving both genetics and environment. People are born with the biological vulnerability to the disorder rather than the disorder itself. OCD can develop at any period from early childhood through adulthood, with between one-third and one-half of cases developing in childhood or adolescence. The disease can be triggered by environmental factors and stress (as in Alicia's case), or by growing up in an exceptionally rigid household, or by pregnancy and childbirth, or by infections such as strep throat.

What is happening? PET (positron emission tomography) scans have revealed the OCD patients have hyperactivity in three brain regions: the thalamus and anterior cingulate, the orbital frontal cortex, and the basal ganglia. As well as being abnormally active, these three brain regions show an unusual unity in OCD patients, especially in moments of anxiety. At such times, all three brain regions will simultaneously shift into overdrive, with neurons firing everywhere. It appears that the root problem is with the processing center or filtering station that coordinates the three, the caudate nucleus. When this processing/filtering center is functioning normally, shifting from one thought to the next is easy and natural. Any "extra" or misdirected thoughts are filtered out automatically. This is crucial because strangely enough, the biggest task for the brain isn't making its neurons "go"; it's making them "stop." But for a person with OCD, not enough "stops" are given; certain thoughts that should be filtered out are not. The person becomes physically incapable of filtering them out, no matter how much they want to or how hard they try.

And they do try very hard, which is how the "compulsiveness" part of OCD comes in. To replace or suppress the thoughts and/or control the anxiety that accompanies them, the individual develops rituals. A ritual may be a physical act such as hand washing, ordering, or checking; or it may be a mental act such as counting, making lists, or repeating words silently. No matter what form compulsions take, their purpose is always the same: to neutralize the thoughts and control anxiety.

Some people may experience temporary relief from these rituals, and so be able to function at work or school. In the long term, these rituals are counterproductive in stopping the thoughts or providing lasting relief from anxiety. With the increase of frantic messages to the already clogged processing/filtering center, the jam gets worse and anxiety rises. This causes the malfunctioning areas of the brain to become more hyperactive and more "stuck." In a vicious circle, the frightened OCD patient responds with still more compulsive behavior.

As the sufferer becomes increasingly consumed by efforts to suppress the uncontrollable thoughts, he or she becomes increasingly unable to engage in normal activity. Difficulties with attention, concentration, and sleep appear. Exhaustion sets in, and the condition worsens. Usually intrusive thoughts and the compulsions they lead to are accompanied by a high degree of anxiety and/or depression. Alicia is at this point experiencing both anxiety and the beginnings of depression.

Alicia had been descending slowly into the depths of depression, but now she plummeted.

Sleep was impossible; lying awake and alone with the thoughts was likewise impossible. She insisted on "sleeping" with her mother, something she hadn't done since she was very young. The child in her still believed that Mommy would protect her against all dangers, and she was absorbed some comfort from her mother's presence. She was terrified of being left alone.

In the dark of the long night (had nights always been so long?) she tried to talk to her mother. Perhaps talking it out would silence the thoughts, or at least distract her from them for a little while. She could not describe what the thoughts were really like though. She simply didn't have the vocabulary. She instead tried to describe how they made her feel.

"It's like my heart is numb," she began, referring to the deadness inside.

"Is this a physical problem that needs a doctor?"

"No." Obviously this wasn't going to work. Next she tried to explain her fears of losing her faith.

Mrs. Adams replied, "Don't worry about your faith – your faith is a gift of God." Alicia felt snubbed. She knew that was the correct answer and the one Dad would have approved of, but it didn't match what she was going through. It was the right answer to the wrong question.

They continued talking, but not communicating, for awhile before Mrs. Adams went to sleep. She was a good mother who was very sorry that her child was so upset. But she still didn't understand why. And Alicia could not explain what she didn't understand herself.

So she lay awake and listened to her mother's breathing, and that was perhaps the most comfort she could have received.

———⋈———

People with OCD often feel that they are all alone, and that no one could possibly understand. Like Alicia, they are ashamed of their inability to control their own minds, and may fear being thought "crazy" or "silly." Some hide their illness, suffering in silence for months or years at a time. If they are willing to tell somebody about their problems, they risk being misunderstood. Societal stereotypes of mental illness are generally based on much rarer disorders such as schizophrenia! The less dramatic illness of OCD may go unrecognized, even by healthcare professionals. The average OCD sufferer sees three or four doctors and spends nine years seeking treatment before receiving an accurate diagnosis. Too many doctors have not been trained to identify OCD or supply the proper treatment.

And remember, OCD often begins in childhood or adolescence. Young teenagers like Alicia find it extremely difficult to communicate their experiences and feelings clearly enough for parents and teachers to distinguish their serious depressions from adolescent angst. Their misery is dismissed as "just a stage." As a recent article has concluded: "Most of the nearly three million adolescents struggling with depression never get the help they need because of prejudice about mental illness, inadequate mental-health resources and widespread ignorance about how emotional problems can wreck young lives."

© Copyright 2005
Alicia Adams
40 Peony Ave Apt. 14
Middletown PA 17057

Chapter Two: Fighting the Shadow

Mr. Adams was a very intellectual man who prided himself on his wide knowledge and powers of discernment. His belief system was unique, formulated by his independent studies rather than the received teachings of others. He never failed to critique the beliefs of others, and never saw any reason to refrain from doing so in Alicia's hearing. He did not believe that his children should take the teachings of others as unquestioned truth, any more than he did so himself. He always told Alicia that she should not go by what he said or by what her teachers said, but by the Bible. How a child of fourteen could possibly be qualified to evaluate the conflicting teachings of adults, he did not explain.

He generally talked to her as if she were an adult, about things he was interested in, things he was reading and learning, and things he wondered about. He seldom, if ever, talked with her about anything in her own life, or at least not without trying to make a parallel between it and something in his studies. The unintended message was that the Alicia's real life as a fourteen-year-old was of no interest, that she was in fact very secondary to whatever was going on in his mind at the moment. She might not have taken it that way – or cared as much - if she had had friends her own age who could acknowledge her everyday life as important. But as it was, she believed herself to be unacceptable to other kids, to be unacceptable as a kid.

So she counterfeited a maturity she did not possess, and not surprisingly, did so rather badly. As a most pretentious pretender, entirely too eager to think and talk about "intellectual" subjects, her mental life became increasingly divorced from the real world of the young high school student: the world where she would never be accepted. Her mind was a refuge for her, a place where rejection and loneliness could not come, a place where she would always be safe... until the thoughts had come, and turned her mind into a war zone.

It was thus as natural for Alicia to expect her father to come up with a solution from his vast reservoir of intellect, as it was natural for him to attempt to do so. Time after time she would get him up in the middle of the night, demanding that he somehow "talk" the thoughts away. So he sat up with her, talked to her, prayed with her, tried to distract her from the issue, urged faith as a cure for lack of faith, assured her of his unconditional love – he did everything he could think of to help his anxious child. But for all the effect he had on Alicia's thoughts, he might as well have been arguing with a broken leg.

Logic is no defense against intrusive thoughts; however, Alicia is not alone in her belief that her obsessions can and must be resolved by some magnificent chain of reasoning, some answer she's not thought of, some feat of mental gymnastics. This conviction is found in many people who have the form of OCD known as the "purely obsessive" type. The term "purely obsessive" is misleading as these OCD patients are not without compulsive behavior; rather, they are engaging in a distinct kind of compulsive behavior: "the non-observable, mental 'pushing away' of the thought, avoiding the recurrence of the thought, or attempting to solve the question or undo the threat that the thought presents."

This is exactly what is happening with Alicia: she feels so threatened by her intrusive thoughts that she is driven to great efforts to "undo" or invalidate them. Repetitive prayers are one weapon against the thoughts, as she pleads desperately for them to be taken away. A more complicated compulsion is her urge to disprove the thoughts, to "argue" with them. She throws all her intellectual energy into making a "case" against the thoughts. Yet all the time, the thoughts keep repeating themselves; they never change, they never respond to her reasoning – or to that of Mr. Adams, who has now been drawn into Alicia's compulsive mental ritual.

It is also very common for people with OCD to enlist their family members in carrying out their compulsive behaviors. Initially, Mr. Adams was a willing participant in Alicia's mental compulsion; he too expected Alicia's "doubts" to be resolved through reason. When the non-rational character of her thoughts became apparent, he said to his daughter, "I don't understand this type of argument, where there's nothing on the other side!" Without realizing it, he had stumbled upon the key feature of compulsive mental rituals – there is nothing on the other side. No matter what Alicia does to try and overcome her thoughts, there is nothing that will respond or even take notice.

Imagine a very unusual kind of debate. On one side there is a broken record that repeats the same statement over and over; on the other side there is a person, working frantically to disprove the statement with every kind of logic at her disposal, and becoming increasingly frantic when the record player does not "change its mind." Insane? This is the situation Alicia finds herself in. She feels that she is "losing the argument," and she is blind to the fact that there is no way to "win" over an unreal, unreasoning "opponent." She and other purely obsessionals falsely believe: "that there is a way to turn off the obsession, and that they just have to keep obsessing until they hit upon that way. If they can find 'the answer', the right thought, then the obsessing will just vanish completely."

But these unfortunate people are fighting a shadow. No matter what questions are answered or what mental gymnastics are gone through, the intrusive thoughts will not go away. Remember, the root problem in OCD is that the brain's processing/filtering center has become jammed, and the three brain regions it orchestrates have reacted with hyperactivity. One doctor explains this with an illustration that hints at the frustration experienced: "It's like having your car stuck in a ditch. You spin and spin and spin your wheels, but without traction you can't get out of that ditch. The wheels are spinning fast and using up tons of energy, but the car's still not going anywhere."

Each of the three hyperactive brain regions has a distinct role to play in the development of OCD. The thalamus and anterior cingulate are a part of the limbic system, which plays a key role in our emotions, anxiety, and basic drives. The limbic system is concerned with hygiene, territorial order, sex, and aggression. Most, through not all, obsessions are directly connected to one or more of those issues.

Basic drives originate in the limbic system but are regulated by the cortex. The orbital frontal cortex is responsible for our impulse control (keeping us from acting on every drive), emotional self-regulation (controlling the natural responses of the limbic system), and control of attention (determining what to focus on and how much). It is central to "the processing, expression, and regulation of emotional information" and is involved in emotional memory, the imprint of emotionally significant experiences on our brains. Most significantly for persons with OCD, the orbital frontal cortex is responsible for scanning the *environment for danger and planning ways to avoid harm. Harm avoidance is all-consuming for someone with OCD.*

The basal ganglia may be the most critical of the three. The basal ganglia develops "habit memories" for behaviors we have practiced repeatedly, so that we can carry out these habits easily, without much thought. Riding a bike takes a lot of concentration at first, but becomes second nature because the habit memory is stamped upon the brain. Unfortunately, compulsive rituals also become fixed. As OCD sufferers frantically repeat their rituals – whether physical or mental - their habit memory is strengthened and they become still more locked into their compulsions. The downward spiral continues.

The Adams family returned home exhausted and sick at heart. Alicia continued to be unable to sleep nights, even though her mom had begun giving her nighttime cold medicine to knock her out for a little while. She began to have trouble eating and keeping food down, as well. And she cried uncontrollably, especially in the mornings. Clearly something had to be done.

Mr. and Mrs. Adams recognized that Alicia had been unhappy ever since the beginning of the school year. Perhaps it had been a mistake to enroll her in public school. They began looking into those Christian schools in the area that had high school programs. Alicia, still clinging to her childish belief that her brilliant father was certain to come up with a solution to her thoughts, became convinced that a new environment was all it would take to get rid of them. After all, Dad thought so. It might have been power of suggestion, but it was the first ray of hope she'd had in what felt like forever.

The Adams searched diligently and found a school that seemed suitable and which was willing to take Alicia mid-year. It was while arrangements were being made for this transfer that the Adams became more aware of Alicia's "self-absorption," as they termed it. When they thought of what they wanted in a school for Alicia, at the top of the list was the chance to make some real friends. However, Alicia refused to even hope for this, believing that she would only be disappointed and hurt. "I don't *want* friends. All I want is to be left alone," she protested. It seemed a quite reasonable request to her. Maybe she didn't deserve to have friends, but surely anyone had the right to go to school without being teased and tormented. Why was it, she wondered, that someone who asked as little of life as she did couldn't have even that small wish granted?

Alicia did not even attempt to explain this to her parents, so all they knew was that Alicia seemed determined to live her life as a hermit. Didn't she care about anybody besides herself? Why was it that she hadn't even tried to make friends at her last school? They were trying so hard to help but it didn't seem to make any difference to her. Maybe she didn't even care about them! Did they do something terribly wrong? Why was their daughter like this?

In the midst of these anxieties, Mr. Adams received a visitor. Mr. Batdorf, like Mr. Adams, was interested in theology and lacking in a church. The two men began their conversation pleasantly enough. Then Mr. Batdorf happened to spy a Simpson comic book belonging to Alicia's younger brother. Immediately he turned on Mr. Adams: Didn't he know how unchristian it was to watch Simpsons? Only a very bad father would allow a child to read such a comic book! The invectives continued until Mr. Batdorf left in disgust.

At another time, Mr. Adams might have dismissed Mr. Batdorf as the legalistic jerk that he was. Not now. Mr. Batdorf has unknowingly hit him in a tender spot. Maybe it was true that he was a bad father. His daughter had so many problems…

That night, Mr. Adams slept fitfully, unable to forget the condemnation of Mr. Batdorf, and worrying about his child. Alicia couldn't sleep at all, but managed to stay in her bed this time, waiting eagerly for the morning. For the next day, she was to go to her new school for the first time!

She was so enthusiastic that she got up before her alarm went off (unheard of for her) and was dressed and downstairs with time to spare. Then she burst into sudden tears, surprising even herself. She just couldn't hold herself together another second. Ever since she had become ill, this often happened in the mornings. In between sobs, she confessed that once again, she hadn't slept all night. This, too, was all too common.

Mrs. Adams's patience was exhausted. They'd gone to a lot of trouble to make this new school happen for Alicia and she didn't even care! What was wrong with this child? Frustrated, she went to get her husband. Alicia called to her mother, "Don't wake Dad, I'll be all right," but Mrs. Adams didn't listen.

Left alone, Alicia took a book and sat down, figuring that a little reading would calm her down. Almost instantly, her tears began to slow down. Since she was still hopeful about the school day, it is likely she would have had herself under reasonably good control in a matter of minutes. She could still have gotten ready in plenty of time to meet the bus.

She wasn't given a chance though. Mr. Adams came running down stairs, angrier than Alicia had ever seen him. He screamed at her to get up and get out the door RIGHT NOW. This was going to be a hard day! Alicia was just making it harder! She had to get going! Terrified, Alicia tried to obey. Lately, she just couldn't seem to move as fast as usual though. Everything seemed to take more effort. On this morning in particular, her hands just weren't working as they should. She couldn't get her coat to zip up.

Mr. Adams didn't see this. He only saw that she was standing still (as her shaking hands fumbled with the zipper) and still crying. He screamed even louder for her to GO and to her he didn't even look like her father anymore, more like some deranged lunatic. Alicia somehow managed to move past him and out the door, still unzipped up and completely unprepared to face the school day. "I hate you," was her cry of ultimate despair. If even her father had rejected her, what hope was left?

She ran to the bus stop and stood there crying for what seemed like a century before the bus arrived. (It was probably more like three minutes.) The bus went to another school first, and there Alicia looked out and saw her father watching her and looking sad. She looked away angrily. How dare he try and guilt-trip her now after he had frightened her so much! He wasn't going to manipulate *her* that way.

Alicia cried the entire way to school. Once inside, however, she had a better day than she'd had in months. The kids were welcoming but not overwhelmingly so, letting her get adjusted at her own pace. Alicia was actually able to concentrate on what was happening, at least half the time. Her thoughts came and went, sometimes overpowering her and causing her to hide her tears in her book, but leaving her alone long enough to enjoy a part of the day. That for her was wonderful progress. She would have considered it a very good day, if she hadn't been dreading coming home.

Eventually she had to though. Her father asked her gruffly, "So, do you still hate me?" and she burst into tears again, unable to look at him. Their relationship would never be the same. Her trust had been lost.

> *Alicia is showing classic signs of clinical depression, a condition experienced by 70% of OCD sufferers. She can't sleep or eat normally. Her tension leads to vomiting. She cries uncontrollably. She finds morning to be the hardest part of the day. She has "psychomotor retardation" – she can't coordinate her movements as easily or as fast as usual and finds everything takes more effort than it should.*
>
> *Her parents have been amazing up until now. A person with depression is very difficult to live with, especially when no one knows what's really wrong. Now her disease is taking a toll on them too. They've tried everything to help their child and it hasn't worked. They've been overwhelmed by Alicia's increased neediness, as well as*

their own feelings of helplessness, frustration, and fear that that they are somehow responsible. They haven't been getting adequate sleep. They are drained and discouraged, with little patience left for Alicia. Their reaction is only human, but for Alicia very threatening.

Because of her OCD (which neither she nor her parents know about yet) she is in a vulnerable state, incredibly sensitive to any threat in her environment. She experienced the threat more intensely at the time, and the imprint upon her emotional memory was unusually deep. For over a year to follow, the memory of that morning would come upon her at unexpected times, bringing back all the shock and betrayal of a child discovering her parents might fail her just when she needs them most. The trauma of that memory would fade only when it was replaced by worse ones.

Despite the bumpy start, the new school was a haven for Alicia. It was small, with about two dozen students in each grade: no crowds, no confusing hallways. The other kids were "nice" - they didn't swear or make fun of her or shove her in the hallways. More importantly, they were an unusually accepting, flexible group, more unified than high school classes generally are. They were willing, even eager, to include a new student in their class, but they were also able to respect that student's hesitancy and not push for more. Alicia, or any unhappy child for that matter, could not have asked for a better chance of making a fresh start.

Combined with her own expectation of getting rid of the thoughts, the results were remarkable. The thoughts gradually diminished, her appetite returned, and she began to sleep through the night once more. The crying stopped, and Alicia became filled with joy, confident that she had beaten the thoughts and was back to her old self. She and her parents agreed that the new school was a huge success!

If OCD is neurological, how come the symptoms can disappear spontaneously, without treatment? Alicia's recovery is likely to be caused by a combination of two factors: 1) the placebo effect (persons with OCD are often highly suggestible) and 2) a dramatic reduction in the stress that triggered the disorder. It is quite common for OCD symptoms to wax and wane with stress.

Once "cured," Alicia resumed most of her former patterns of thinking and interacting, developed during middle school. Despite her classmates' willingness to include her, she remained on the fringes of things at school, convinced this was where she belonged. Her response to their overtures was sporadic and often minimal. Most of the time, she didn't give the other girls much reason to take the trouble to befriend her. Yet they did, content to get little in return. It would take many years for Alicia to realize that their attitude was the exact opposite of what she had experienced in sixth grade. In the meantime, their kindness meant more to Alicia than she cared to admit, even to herself. Isolation had been familiar and safe. To move beyond that involved a radical shift in her approach to life – a huge risk!

Not only that, she discovered that she didn't even know *how* to respond to the other girls. Despite their efforts to include her, she always felt that she was out of step with her classmates, that there was a difference between her and them that should not be there. In a way this was true. During the four years preceding her enrollment, she had been so withdrawn that she had missed out on normal opportunities for social development. She came to ninth grade with the social development of a fourth- or fifth-grader at best. She didn't know how teenagers related to each other, and she had just enough awareness of her ignorance to be fearful of making mistakes. She didn't realize *why* she was unable to relate to the others as smoothly as they did.

Most of the time, she was an observer rather than a participant in the life of the classroom. She did enjoy watching the other kids – she came home everyday with stories of how so-and-so said this and so-and-so did that, which she eagerly related to her mother. Relating these rather commonplace occurrences, she felt as though she really was a part of "our class," or, to use her new favorite word, "us."

© Copyright 2005
Alicia Adams
40 Peony Ave Apt. 14
Middletown PA 17057

Chapter Three:
The Valley of Deepest Darkness

As ninth grade came to an end, the other girls in Alicia's class eagerly made plans to do things over the summer, assuring each other they'd probably be together about as much as in the school year. About half were in the same youth group, which made things easier, as did the fact that most of them had been friends since childhood and their parents were accustomed to their being in and out of each others' houses. But Alicia said nothing, and no one said anything to her. Silently she resigned herself to a mostly solitary summer. Wasn't that what she wanted — to be left alone? Yet in the last few months, she'd grown to like many of these girls, and she wished that she could be "one of them." But she did not believe that would ever be.

Alicia spent the summer volunteering in a nursing home and reading many books. She seldom saw anybody from school; nobody ever came to visit. It did not surprise her. And she was not at all unhappy; she was very accustomed to her own company and used to amusing herself with her books and with her own thoughts. The experiences of the previous winter had not taught her the dangers of living too much in her own mind. Rather, her restoration to "her real self" had made the life of the mind more valuable to her. She was like an athlete who, once his broken leg is healed, does not seek new interests but determines to throw himself into sports with all the more pleasure.

Fall came, and Alicia entered tenth grade with confidence, even cockiness. This year was going to be so different from last year. She was in her great new school where she felt so secure. And after all, she was older and wiser now than when she'd had those silly thoughts; hadn't she "grown spiritually" (a phrase she'd picked up at school) through that experience, so much that she would never have to go through it again? She felt very proud of herself for having gotten "victory" (another new word) over the thoughts. She didn't think anyone else in her class had ever fought such a battle. (She was probably right about that!)

Her vanity lasted into November and then reality – that is, her disorder - caught up to her. About a year after her thoughts first began, they returned suddenly and worse than before. Alicia was confused. This wasn't supposed to ever happen again! And not in her new school! Had she done something wrong - was God punishing her with these thoughts? Or was it some kind of spiritual warfare – was the devil fighting God for her soul? She prayed fervently – frantically, actually – hoping to bring the battle to a quick conclusion. But nothing seemed to happen.

Life was going on all around her, but she was caught up in her private battle, which now occupied every waking hour. She tried to distract herself, or at least comfort herself, with familiar things, especially familiar books. Even while at a bookstore with her father, she sought out a book she had at home and had read about ten times before. She was sitting and trying in vain to focus on it when her father caught her.

He erupted in the car on the way home, outraged that she would waste such a good opportunity of finding new books by reading one she had at home. Alicia listened with a dullness he mistook for sullenness. Altogether, it did not set the stage well for Alicia's confession that once again she was struggling with "doubts." She still hadn't come up with a more accurate label; she still couldn't bring herself to try and explain what the thoughts were really like.

They were right back where they started from, and Mr. Adams was furious. The brilliant solution, the new school, was not the cure-all they had expected it to be; Alicia had exactly the same "doubts" and depression that she had had before. She'd put them to all that trouble and expense for nothing! Did she want to change schools again now, just on a whim? No, she didn't? (Mr. Adams seemed to forget that it was he, and not Alicia, who had suggested changing schools in the first place; she had not connected her illness with school until he had taught her to.)

Once Alicia's obsessions began again, she very quickly moved into the same compulsive behaviors she had practiced before. This time, however, her father was not sympathetic, but resentful and often hostile. In his very rational way, he was determined to pin down the reason for the thoughts. Alicia tried to tell him that there was no reason, that the thoughts were not rational. He could not understand or accept this, and wondered aloud (in what seemed to Alicia to be a <u>very</u> threatening manner) if she were hiding something from him. And why hadn't she made any real friends in the time she'd been in school? Why was she lost in her thoughts all the time? What was wrong with her?

He kept pushing her for answers that would make sense to him, and she had none to give him. She didn't know why she was the way she was, and she didn't like it either. From the beginning, she had been confused and frightened, and he was terrifying and confusing her more every day. Alicia was already lost in the maze of her own thoughts, and trying to follow her father's attempts at reasoning with her was just too taxing, especially as she became more drained by her illness. Half the time, she hadn't the slightest idea what he was trying to say. The feeling was no doubt mutual.

Alicia grew sicker and sicker. She couldn't sleep; she couldn't eat; and she was vomiting several times a day from the unbearable tension that seemed to permeate her body. She couldn't focus in school and her grades dropped. Her depression was all-consuming; she could take no pleasure in anything. Her life was a misery to her and she was wracked with fear as the thoughts continued to grow worse. She was fighting so hard to maintain her faith under incredibly difficult circumstances, and what if she lost the fight?

Mr. Adams was incapable of sympathy. He saw Alicia's fears that the thoughts would rob of her faith as evidence not of illness but of poor theology, an offense to him at all times and especially in one he'd taught. Hadn't he always told her that faith was given by God and that none of the elect would be lost? Was his child an Armenian? So instead of comfort or empathy, she was accused of unbelief – the very thing she feared so much! The situation was hopeless: if she feared losing her faith that meant she was losing it, and so she became more fearful. It was a vicious circle that did nothing but damage her further.

The fact that the fresh wounds were inflicted by her father made it so much harder to bear. She reasoned that if he rejected her, all hope must surely be gone. And there seemed to be reason enough to conclude that she had forfeited his love forever.

She'd come to him in a panic attack, crying, "Dad, I'm so afraid!"

And he screamed at her, "What are you afraid of? You're afraid of losing your faith! Instead of basing your assurance on the blood of Christ, you base it on the up and down of your faith!" And on and on until she ran from him in terror, usually to the bathroom where she would once again throw up. Strangely it was only after vomiting that she felt even slightly better.

Other times he was somewhat gentler but just as condemning. "I've taught you about the grace of God, but you don't really believe that, do you? You still want your salvation to depend upon something in your mind." Alicia nodded in despair. It must be true. She must be unregenerate. Yet she had really thought that she did believe all she was taught. In fact she'd been absolutely certain of it. But these thoughts were undoing everything she thought was certain.

A whole month had gone by and still she was determined never to succumb. She clung as tightly as she could to what little faith she had left, and continued going to her father and begging him to help her. Despite clear evidence that nothing he said was helping, she still felt compelled to confess her evil thoughts to him, and try to get him to say something that would make the thoughts go away. It was her only hope. And so she endured his accusations and his anger. She must deserve it, after all. Just like she must deserve to be tormented with these thoughts…

"I see no evidence of faith in you at all, at any time," he yelled. "You don't care about anybody but yourself. You never volunteer to help out around the house, you hole yourself up in your own room, you don't have any friends. You couldn't care less about mom and me and what we've gone through with you. This 'faith' you talk about is only in your mind; it has nothing to do with your behavior."

She thought it over and decided he was right. She didn't know how she could be a Christian and be this way. Yet when she said so, she was again accused of unbelief. Christians trusted in Christ alone and not their behavior, and Alicia was "absolutely infuriating" in coming to him again when he'd clearly had enough of talking to her.

Alicia was cut to the heart. Moreover, she was very confused. To begin with, Dad had always said that morality was not Christianity and that salvation was by faith in the true gospel. Then he turned around and said she must not have faith because she wasn't good. When she agreed with him, then she wasn't trusting in Christ. Whatever she did was wrong. Was there ever anyone as wretched as herself?

She never spoke to anybody at school anymore; she couldn't tell anybody about the thoughts and it was impossible to think or talk about anything else. She still tried hard to do her work, but just couldn't manage to stay focused. Several times she had vomited at school and had to come home. Other times she had had to retreat to the quietness of the bathroom to get a hold of herself so that she would not cry or scream in front of the others. Over and over she'd pray to be forgiven and relieved of these awful thought. Now there were times when she could no longer even pray. This scared her still more, as it seemed evidence that she was lost. She described the feeling to her father, who was sick of hearing about all that she thought and felt.

He finally asked in exasperation, "Why do you even want to be a Christian?"

Alicia had never considered such a question in her life. The possibility of not wanting to be a Christian had not even crossed her mind, and she couldn't really think about it now. Severe depression is not conducive to grasping radically new ideas. Therefore, her reply sounded weak even to her own ears. "It just seems that life would be really meaningless without God."

Alicia's depression grew to the point where she was actually considering ending her life. She was very frightened that she could even think such a thing. She didn't want to tell anybody. But when her parents told her that they were going out for the evening and leaving her all alone in the house, she knew she had to.

Her timing was unfortunate, as usual. Mr. Adams was already angry at her, as he was all the time these days. He had long since forgotten, if indeed he had ever known, that she was *a child*, still dependent on her parent's love and approval, and was now a very sick child who hadn't slept or eaten normally in several weeks. Her sufferings were disregarded; he was only interested in how he could condemn her further. At the moment, he had just been scolding her for not speaking to anybody at school that day. "I don't really think you're shy," he said. "It's just a way of talking about you. You really just don't care about anybody else."

Alicia, like many depressed people (adults and teens), had said such things to herself before. It is hard for those with depressive illnesses not to blame themselves for their inability to do the things that normal people do. It was now to be even harder. Her father's words were the more devastating because they weren't spoken in anger, but in resignation. He had really come to believe that his daughter was that unloving. His ignorance of her underlying problems, combined with his habitual disregard for anyone's feelings, had robbed him of any possibility of insight into her condition.

Mr. Adams continued, "Your mom and I are going over to the Limroths' for Bible study. You can stay here all by yourself, since that seems to be what contents you."

Alicia's face fell. He noted that with rising anger. "Why you looking sad?" he barked.

"I don't think you should leave me alone tonight," she said, hoping he wouldn't make her say why.

"Why?" he demanded.

"Because I've been thinking of killing myself." She said it with a certain dramatic flair, reflecting not impudence but desperation. "I can't live without God. All the happiness I ever had was when I believed in Him."

"So all the rest of your life has to be just like your past? You're going to stay up there in that room forever?" Mr. Adams challenged.

Alicia was in such a state that she was incapable of following his reasoning, or any reasoning for that matter. She sobbed out weakly, "I don't like changes." This was true, but hardly the point. How could she make him see that the life was condemned to was no life at all? It was nothing but misery for her and for all who were forced to deal with her. Her parents would most definitely be better off without her. Everyone would.

How should a parent, or anybody for that matter, react to the words: "I've been thinking of killing myself"? According to the American Association of Sucidology, one should:
- *Be direct. Talk openly and matter-of-factly about suicide.*
- *Be willing to listen. Allow expressions of feelings. Accept the feelings.*
- *Be non-judgmental. Don't debate whether suicide is right or wrong, or feelings are good or bad. Don't lecture on the value of life.*
- *Get involved. Become available. Show interest and support.*
- *Don't dare him or her to do it.*
- *Don't act shocked. This will put distance between you.*
- *Don't be sworn to secrecy. Seek support.*
- *Offer hope that alternatives are available but do not offer glib reassurance.*
- *Take action. Remove means, such as guns or stockpiled pills.*

- *Get help from persons or agencies specializing in crisis intervention and suicide prevention.*

The most important thing to remember is that someone considering suicide is desperate, and crying for help. The last thing he or she needs is to be condemned and scorned.

Mr. Adams handled Alicia's suicidal thoughts about as badly as any parent could possibly handle them without actually telling the child to do the deed. He ridiculed her for fearing change. He moralized on the selfishness of suicide. He treated her grief with complete contempt. But there was one thing that hurt more than anything else.

Her parents did allow her to accompany them to the Limroths' – although to Alicia, it appeared that her father was less interested in keeping her from committing suicide than in continuing his tirade against her in the car. On the way he stopped to buy her an ice cream sundae. (Mr. Adams was always trying to get his daughter to eat more; and he generally considered food a substitute for the emotional warmth he was incapable of.)

Alicia had no appetite. Yet she took the sundae and forced down one bite. Her tense stomach rebelled, and before she knew what would happen she had vomited all over her clothes. Fresh tears began to flow as she reached yet another level of pain. No matter how painful her existence became, it seemed like there was always another level she could sink to.

Vomiting was by no means unusual for her in those days. What devastated her was the disgust in her father's eyes. In that moment when she was already wracked with self-loathing it appeared to her that the disgust was not for the vomit, but for her alone. She sobbed incoherently that she didn't realize she would throw up, that she was sorry...

Mr. Adams' voice shook with what she took for more anger, though perhaps it was really grief. "Why didn't you open the car door and throw up outside instead of on yourself? I would have thought that anybody would have had that much instinct for self-preservation."

He started the car again. Not another word was said to her.

© Copyright 2005
Alicia Adams
40 Peony Ave Apt. 14
Middletown PA 17057

Chapter Four:
The Faint Dawn of Hope

At this point, Mr. and Mrs. Adams were forced to face the fact that they were not going to be able to solve Alicia's problem on their own. Mr. Adams called his friend Robert Austin, hoping for some guidance from the older man. Mr. Austin listened to Mr. Adams' account and concluded that he too would be out of his depth. He advised the Adams to take her to Lee Fischer, the Minister of Pastoral Care at a nearby church.

Lee Fischer had a strong background in psychology and counseling, as well as in theology, and the Adams had finally come to accept that Alicia was having a psychological problem. Indeed, Mrs. Adams had thought so since Alicia's first depression; however, she had been rather left out of things as Alicia and Mr. Adams both became caught up in Alicia's mental compulsion. This was by her own choice. "Your father is better at abstract thinking," she told Alicia, excusing herself.

―◆―

Some readers may have been asking, "Where was Alicia's mother when all of this was going on? Why didn't she do anything to protect her young and vulnerable daughter?" Alicia was to ask those questions many times as she grew older. There are no satisfactory answers, yet the phenomenon is not uncommon. Many children have been far more abused than Alicia, while a mother looked on and did nothing. The fear of getting involved can be stronger even than the impulse to protect one's child.

Alicia met with Lee Fischer in his office, while Mr. and Mrs. Adams waited outside. First, Lee verified the information he had been given by Alicia's parents – that is, that Alicia was experiencing "doubts," depression, and suicidal thoughts. With only slight hesitation, Alicia acknowledged that this was all true. She had been nervous about this meeting, but Lee's calm, matter-of-fact manner helped put her at ease. Alicia had noticed before that Lee "talked like a book," meaning that his words were always carefully chosen and considered. He spoke as one who expected his words to have a significant effect on his listeners and wanted it to be for good.

A year before Alicia had tried to tell her father about the thoughts, but she never actually told him much. She didn't have to because he had been so quick to jump in and speak, quite eloquently, on the subject of doubts and faith in general. He had continued to do so throughout the two depressions. It was what Alicia expected of him.

Lee took an entirely different approach. He asked Alicia a question that neither she nor her parents had considered relevant before – just *how* and *when* her "doubts" had begun. Alicia had never told anybody, because it still seemed too crazy to her, but now she was past caring. She just wanted help. So she told him the whole story, from the very beginning, while he listened and did not once interrupt.

She told him how, one night when she was praying, she had a thought come into her head from somewhere else, and how she thought at first that she was under satanic attack. She told him how the thought had gotten worse, gone away, then come back worse than before. And she told him how nothing, nothing could ever silence the thoughts. Not prayers or reasoning or talking to her dad. She told him that at times she was afraid she must really "mean" the thoughts (or else why would she keep having them?), and that must mean she wasn't a Christian. She told him how scared she was and how miserable, how she couldn't eat and sleep any more.

Lee Fischer listened to the whole story in a nearly impassive silence. Then he explained to Alicia that what she was experiencing was an intrusive thought pattern. She had described it very well, he said. Many people, like her, initially thought their intrusive thoughts were the voices of angels or demons, but that wasn't true. The intrusive thoughts were instead caused by a neurological problem that was medically treatable – a problem called obsessive-compulsive disorder. "Don't spiritualize it," he cautioned Alicia. "These thoughts aren't coming from you or from any supernatural being. They're coming from a disordered brain. You can't control it. But these thoughts aren't reality, Alicia."

Without mentioning names, he told her about someone else he had diagnosed with the condition. This was a woman who had just given birth to her first child. She became consumed with thoughts that she would kill her baby. Lee Fischer knew this woman, and he knew that she would never kill her baby, but she herself was consumed with fear and guilt. "Once those thoughts get implanted in your reality, they're very hard to get out. But there is hope, Alicia. You can get help."

Alicia is extraordinarily blessed, to have a pastor who was capable of diagnosing her condition and dealing with it in a reality-based way. Many churches do not have such a person available. In fact, all too many Christians are uncomfortable with the very concept of mental illness and may even deny the existence of such illnesses. Rather than accept the reality of what is, they escape into a "Christian" fantasy of what they think should be.

Christians who are not reality-based make a false dichotomy between general revelation (truth in nature, discovered through observation and reason) and special revelation (truth from the Bible). General revelation is downplayed and distrusted as being "secular" while the Bible is held up as the only "spiritual" reality.

In actual practice, we are all dependent on general revelation for most of the skills and knowledge we use in our daily lives; the Bible is only a small part of the reality we face. In order to function in the real world and maintain the false dichotomy, life itself is divided into areas where it is "all right" to accept general revelation and areas where it is not. The false division between "sacred" and "spiritual" is now more deeply entrenched, extending even to an artificial division of the person into a "spiritual" part (mind/soul) and a "physical" part (body and brain). In this philosophy of dualism, human problems are rigidly categorized as "physical" or "spiritual."

Mental illness defies such categorization. Effective diagnosis and treatment rests on acknowledging both the impact of the malfunctioning brain on the individual's thoughts, feelings, and behavior AND the influence of the thoughts, feelings, and behavior upon the brain. Although general revelation confirms this relationship, the uncompromising dualist may find it philosophically unacceptable. Clinging to this false doctrine inevitably leads to an unrealistic or "spiritualized" approach to problems such as OCD rather than a reality-based approach.

Only someone who has just been diagnosed with OCD can truly understand what an incredible relief it just to know what is wrong. In a matter of minutes, Pastor Fischer had given Alicia hope again, and a reason to go on living. She wasn't "losing her faith." She wasn't "under satanic attack." The thoughts were NOT coming from her or from the devil! They were caused by a malfunctioning brain, of all things! She took in the news with something like joy – at least, something closer to it than anything she'd felt in a very long time.

Alicia doesn't know it, but she's already taking a step toward getting well. More specifically, she's begun to take the first two steps – the first of "The Four Steps" identified by Dr. Jeffery Schwartz. Since the late 1980s, Dr. Schwartz has been a leading proponent of what he calls "cognitive biobehavioral self-treatment" – OCD patients making themselves well by changing their habitual responses to their obsessions. Remember, the natural inclination of an OCD patient is to use compulsive behavior in an attempt to control their obsessions and anxiety, even though such compulsions can only damage them further. By learning self-treatment, OCD patients stop giving in to their compulsions and find new ways of coping with their obsessions. They do this by changing the way they think about their obsessions - bringing their thoughts in line with reality.

The first of the "Four Steps" is to <u>Re-label</u> – to simply recognize the obsessions and compulsions for what they actually are: not reality, but false messages coming from the brain. Even learning to use the appropriate vocabulary – obsession, compulsion, intrusive thought – helps to put the problem into perspective and robs the compulsions of some of their power. For example, some one who has an obsession with cleanliness and is Re-labeling might learn to say to himself, "I don't really need to wash my hands;

I'm having a compulsive urge to perform the compulsion of washing my hands."

The second step is to <u>Re-attribute</u> the intrusive thoughts to a biochemical imbalance in the brain. Dr. Schwartz says, "The key to our self-directed behavioral therapy approach to treating OCD can be summed up in one sentence: "It's not me--it's my OCD." That is our battle cry. It is a reminder that OCD thoughts and urges are not meaningful, that they are false messages from the brain."

These steps sound really simple, but learning to Re-label and Re-attribute takes time and effort. What is required is a 180-degree turn in the way the person has been thinking about and reacting to an all-consuming problem. Alicia, in particular, is accustomed to thinking of her intrusive thoughts as being a spiritual matter. From the start she has been incorrectly labeling and incorrectly attributing. As she involved her father in her compulsion, he became drawn into her way of thinking and reacting. Not only did he reinforce her incorrect labels and attributions, he added some incorrect labels and attributions of his own in his harsh judgments of Alicia.

Now Lee Fischer is offering them both a new way of looking at the situation – a reality-based way. He doesn't use the language of Dr. Schwartz's "Four Steps" to explicitly teach Alicia to <u>Re-label</u> and <u>Re-attribute</u>; however, by calling her OCD by its right name and warning her not to spiritualize it, he is already helping her to move beyond her false labels and attributions. For now, it is enough.

Lee Fischer called Alicia's parents back into his office and briefly explained the diagnosis. He told them their daughter was suffering from a brain-based mental disorder, with both genetic and environmental factors. He gave his opinion that Alicia's OCD had been triggered by the stress of the sudden transfer from her small private elementary school to a large public high school – a difficult transition for any child. Unfortunately, he did not repeat what he had said to Alicia about the importance of never spiritualizing the problem. He had not recognized the extent to which Mr. Adams had been drawn into Alicia's compulsion.

Alicia had quickly recognized the truth of Lee Fischer's diagnosis because it fit in perfectly with what she herself had experienced and had never been able to talk about. She dimly perceived that she had been wrong in labeling her thoughts "doubts;" for in an inarticulate way, she had known all along that something very strange was happening to her. She was overwhelmed with gratitude that someone had at last figured out what it was.

Mr. Adams, on the other hand, had become so accustomed to thinking of Alicia's depression as a crisis in faith that it was difficult for him to let go of that belief and even more difficult to let go of the negative judgments he'd made about her during the time when they had no idea what was wrong. He had only recently come to accept the idea that Alicia had a "psychological problem," and he had never considered that there might be a neurological basis. He was willing to try the treatment Lee Fischer suggested – counseling and anti-depressant medication – but he was not yet prepared to discard his previous ideas about Alicia and her condition. As a comment on the way home made clear, he did not realize that it even made a difference what he believed.

As he mused on the events of the day, he remarked that some people would think of "intrusive thoughts" as being messages from the devil rather than a chemical problem. Alicia nodded fervently, remembering how she herself had thought so at first – now she knew better! Then Mr. Adams went on to say, "I guess it's really the same."

Wrong! There is a world of difference between "These thoughts are demonic" and "These are intrusive thoughts caused by a malfunctioning brain." The former belief is a false attribution that will exacerbate the OCD person's anxiety and compulsiveness. The latter is a correct attribution that will help him or her get well. This kind of distinction is one the first things someone with OCD needs to learn, but although Alicia was warned about spiritualizing her condition, her father was not.

All too often, counselors overlook the fact that the families of people with OCD may also need to learn to <u>Re-label</u> and <u>Re-attribute</u>. It's tempting to focus all efforts on directly helping "the" patient or counselee, but OCD doesn't just affect the person who has it. The parents (or spouses and/or children) of the person also suffer, especially if they have become caught up in the OCD compulsions. They need to know the truth about the disorder just as much as their loved one does, and they need to know how to support – not undermine - the individual's efforts at self-treatment. The family, not just the individual, needs counseling, especially in the beginning. Everybody needs to be aware of the nature of OCD and the importance of Re-labeling and Re-attributing.

Lee Fischer had told the Adams that the first step to getting help for Alicia was to see a general practitioner. For years, Alicia had gone to Dr. Ridge for her shots and childhood ailments. It seemed strange now to be going to her with this kind of problem. Her tale of being startled by supposed "Satanic attacks" which turned out to be really a brain problem seemed out of place in the bright antiseptic environment of the examining room. Would Dr. Ridge know about intrusive thoughts? Could she help?

After listening to Alicia, Dr. Ridge readily agreed with Pastor Fischer's diagnosis and recommendation of medication. She didn't want to prescribe it herself, however, because she'd had little experience with adolescent psychiatry. To Mrs. Adams, who had accompanied Alicia, she recommended a psychiatrist, Dr. Elnicki, who worked at a nearby mental hospital but saw many outpatients.

Mr. Adams took Alicia to see Dr. Elnicki, and Alicia had to repeat her story once more; by now she was feeling a bit more confident about sharing her experience. She wished her father would not interrupt with his own comments; he was trying to help, but it was making her nervous. She also wished that Dr. Elnicki would look at her instead of at his desk. All the time she was talking, he was busy making notes and paging through a book he had. The book Dr. Elnicki was looking through was the DSM-IV. Just like Lee Fischer and Dr. Ridge, he recognized that Alicia was suffering from OCD and depression. Unlike them, he was going to check carefully to see that she actually met all the criteria. He believed that psychiatry was a science that should be practiced as objectively as humanly possible.

How does Alicia measure up? Check her case history and symptoms against the standard definitions.

Obsessions are defined by the following 4 criteria: oRecurrent and persistent thoughts, impulses, or images are experienced at some time during the disturbance as intrusive and inappropriate and cause marked anxiety and distress. oThe thoughts, impulses, or images are not simply worries about real-life problems. oThe person attempts to suppress or ignore such thoughts, impulses, or images or to neutralize them with some other thought or action. oThe person recognizes that the obsessional thoughts, impulses, or images are a product of his/her own mind (not imposed from without).

Compulsions are defined by the following 2 criteria: oThe person feels driven to perform repetitive behaviors (eg, hand washing, ordering, checking) or mental acts (eg, praying, counting, repeating words silently) in response to an obsession or according to rules that must be applied rigidly. oThe behaviors or mental acts are aimed at preventing or reducing distress or preventing some dreaded event or situation; however, these behaviors or mental acts either are not connected in a realistic way with what they are meant to neutralize or prevent or they are clearly excessive.

- *At some point during the course of the disorder, the person recognizes that the obsessions or compulsions are excessive or unreasonable. This does not apply to children.*
- *The obsessions or compulsions cause marked distress; are time consuming (take more than 1 hour a day); or significantly interfere with the person's normal routine, occupational or academic functioning, or usual social activities or relationships.*

Keeping his eyes fastened on his book and ignoring Mr. Adams, Dr. Elnicki briefly questioned Alicia. One of the questions was confusing: he asked Alicia if she "realized that the thoughts were coming from herself and not from another source." She answered, "Yes," guessing that what he meant was, "did she realize that she wasn't hearing from an angel or a demon." It was a tricky question, really, she thought. She had just learned that the thoughts did not come from *her* but they did come from her brain. It was an important distinction, but one she couldn't quite explain. She figured the doctor knew what she meant, anyway.

Other than that, everything was straightforward. In his detached, unemotional way, Dr. Elnicki listed all Alicia's symptoms, as if he were taking inventory of items in a storehouse. Clearly she met all the criteria for obsessive-compulsive disorder and clinical depression.

Mr. Adams shook his head slowly. "I never realized this was so severe."

That remark was to haunt Alicia. *Never realized?* Throughout two depressions, he'd been the main one she'd talked to about her thoughts. She'd tried every possible way to tell him how she felt. And if her words were not enough, couldn't he use his eyes? She'd been unable to eat or sleep for weeks. She was thinking of killing herself. She was living in a long nightmare. But her own father "never realized it was so severe."

How could such an intelligent man be so completely blind to the sufferings of his own child? Didn't he care about her at all?

© Copyright 2005
Alicia Adams
40 Peony Ave Apt. 14
Middletown PA 17057

Chapter Five: No Quick Fix

Mr. Adams disliked Dr. Elnicki from the first. "Talking to him is like talking to an ATM machine," Mr. Adams complained, perhaps nettled that his own "observations" on Alicia's case had been ignored. It was certainly true that this doctor would never win any prizes for his "bedside" manner, at least not from any of his outpatients; he conserved much of his energy for those patients that were hospitalized. In dealing with the milder, more routine cases he saw as outpatients, he was methodical and exact, but distant and detached. His role was to make diagnoses and prescribe medications. He left it up to others – psychologists and social workers - to provide counseling and other therapy.

Dr. Elnicki reflects widespread changes in the treatment of those with OCD and other mental disorders. Gone are the days of traditional psychoanalysis, when a patient like Alicia might spend "several years of several sessions a week with a highly trained and well-paid analyst" exploring the "unconscious roots" of her intrusive thoughts. An example of what this was like can be found in M. Scott Peck's People of the Lie. His patient, "George," had intrusive thoughts about dying and a compulsion to keep returning to the places where he had had the thoughts. For two years, in twice-weekly sessions, Dr. Peck probed his unhappy childhood, his marital difficulties, and his alienation from his children. The symptoms George actually went into therapy for were downplayed as a mere "smoke screen" for George's "real" problems (as defined by Dr. Peck).

"The theory then," explains Marc Summers, "was that if the underlying psychological problems could be understood, the obsessive compulsive symptoms would vanish. It's ironic that traditional psychoanalysis, far from improving my symptoms, might actually have made them worse. Delving into the 'meaning' of my obsessive thoughts might have encouraged me to attribute significance to them, exacerbating the anxiety they provoked in me and causing me to increase my ritualistic behaviors. The doctor might have convinced me that I had obsessive fear of my plane crashing because I secretly wanted to die, instead of helping me understand that these intrusive thoughts were a meaningless reflection of the imbalance in my brain chemistry."

In the '80s and early '90s, this theory was discredited as the biological basis for OCD began to be understood and effective medications were developed. At the same time, a revolution was taking place in psychiatry as a whole. "Insurance companies and health-maintenance organizations, aiming to reduce costs, seized on drugs as a cheaper alternative to therapy. The care of the mentally ill was fractured: Psychiatrists prescribed pills, and psychotherapy, if provided at all, was done by psychologists or social workers, whose hourly rate undercut that of psychiatrists. Communication between the two is often sporadic, and, as a result, most patients receive inadequate care."

As for Alicia, she had mixed feelings about Dr. Elnicki. She would have liked him to look at her occasionally. On the other hand, his bored demeanor was strangely reassuring. It proved that her case was a routine matter to him; he must have treated tons of patients like her already. Besides, she already knew that a lot of talk didn't help her; Pastor Lee had told her that medication would, and she believed him. Dr. Elnicki wrote her first prescription for Prozac – 10 milligrams each morning.

Prozac is one of several SSRI (selective serotonin reuptake inhibitor) medications, which regulate the amount of serotonin in the brain. Serotonin regulates mood and anxiety and "plays a role in assessing danger in the environment, and, by affecting the rate at which neurons fire, it modulates the activity of different brain regions." The last two are highly significant for OCD patients, as they are hyper-aware of danger and suffer from hyperactivity in three brain regions. Beyond this, the relationship between the serotonin system and the caudate nucleus is not well understood.

The first such medication to be used effectively with OCD patients was Anafranil, in 1986. Anafranil had already been approved as an antidepressant; the pharmaceutical industry sponsored 20 studies in different locations to determine whether OCD patients could also benefit – a controversial move as the biological basis for OCD was just beginning to be recognized. The results were astounding: 70% of those who took the medicine showed dramatic improvement. The experiment was tried again with other types of SSRI medications and they were just as effective.

> The best-known SSRI, Prozac, was introduced in 1987. Not only did it have fewer side effects than older antidepressants, it was much more effective at eliminating (not just managing) depression. PBS Odyssey glowingly reported:
>
> > The results were astonishing. Patients reported feeling 'better than well.' It not only eased their depression, but seemed to give them a new look at themselves. Prozac users felt they were discovering their own true personalities for the first time, uninhibited by a vague weight that had bogged them down before. It seemed to make cautious people more spontaneous, the introverted more outgoing, the timid more confident. In short, it seemed to improve people's personalities, at least in making them more socially attractive.

Alicia had never been able to swallow pills before, but on her first morning taking Prozac, she realized that she'd better learn fast. The little green capsule tasted like chalk dust laced with weed killer, and seemed to make her tongue go numb. She tried taking it in ice cream, but it was no use: somehow the nasty taste just spread itself around the entire bowl, even to parts which she was sure were nowhere near the pill itself. She wondered dismally if every morning in her life would begin with that horrible taste in her mouth. Within a week, though, she was gulping down her medicine with no difficulty.

She got to "practice" twice a day. Because she had not slept properly in so long, Dr. Elnicki had prescribed a second medication as well: one which when combined with Prozac had the "side effect" of drowsiness. It was astonishingly effective. On one occasion, not long after she had begun taken her medications, Alicia slept for twenty hours straight. Mrs. Adams kept coming into her room to make sure she was still breathing. Alicia would sometimes rouse enough to know her mother was there, but she could not open her eyes for more than a second. When she finally did wake up, she remained very groggy for four hours, and then easily drifted off to sleep again after eating. Providentially, the conditions were right for hibernating: a blizzard had ripped through Alicia's home town and shut down her school for over a week - the very week in which she was requiring so much sleep!

Even aside from her spell as a human sloth – a very thirsty one, as she also had a dry mouth – Alicia's first weeks on Prozac were blurred, not only in her memory later on, but even at the time. The experience was indescribably confusing. She could feel that the medication was "doing something," but she couldn't have said, even to herself, precisely what it was she felt. It was so frustrating. If the untreated depression had been like a cage, the cage door was now open and she still could not get out. In some ways she was getting better, but often she felt worse. Her mood had gone from uniformly sad to completely unpredictable. She felt as helpless as a puppet on strings, as her emotions were constantly jerked around from hope to despair, sometimes within a single hour, and from no apparent cause.

Alicia was crying more than ever, but the thoughts were gradually decreasing. The noisy war in her head was being replaced by quietness and emptiness. She felt like a string which had been stretched as tight as it could go, and now had snapped. In some ways this was a relief, but there was a horror to it as well. She didn't know what it meant - the struggle was ending, but had she won or lost? She had been unendurably tense for so long; now she was... not. Not tense. Not having intrusive thoughts. Yet not happy. All her sensations were of negation, of nothingness. She had never realized that she could feel so much like nothing. It seemed that her illness had swallowed up everything that was "her" – there was no Alicia left.

Driving through the blinding snow, the Adams went back to Dr. Elnicki, but learned little from him. He considered Alicia's reactions to her new medications to be quite normal. "Whenever you come out of a depression," he said, "you have to catch up on sleep." Then as an afterthought, "And remember, kids will be kids." That seemed to be the best explanation he had to give them. He was satisfied that Alicia had no significant side effects and advised that she continue to take her medication and begin counseling when it could be arranged – probably after the snowstorm was over. The appointment hardly seemed worth the trip.

In due time, Alicia did begin her counseling appointments with John Havrilla. Mr. Havrilla was not a doctor; he was a clinical social worker who had had a great deal of experience with OCD. Currently, he was counseling many children and youth who, like Alicia, were outpatients of the local mental hospital. Most of his counselees were very young; at fifteen, Alicia was one of his oldest. He was as gentle and soft-spoken as Mr. Rodgers; in fact, his way of speaking and overall demeanor was often very similar to that of the famous children's television personality. Had Alicia been quite herself when she met him, she probably would have considered it a supreme insult to be taken to what was so obviously a "little kids' counselor."

Under the circumstances, however, she was in no mood to insist on her dignity as a nearly-sixteen-year-old. Just like a younger child, she responded to his soothing personality, and felt much better, much more stable, when she was with him. Mr. Havrilla gave her hope. At last there was someone who understood her and her thoughts, who had known other people like her who actually got better again after being sick like this. (Often she felt that there could never be any end to this, that she was always going to be a shell of her former self.) In the storm of her illness, he was a life preserver… her way of keeping in touch with reality.

Mr. Havrilla combined comfort with education about her disorder. Because he was accustomed to working with younger kids, it was automatic for him to provide very simple, not-too-technical explanations. He liked to create special imagery that would enable the child to have a concrete, vivid picture of what was happening to her. He'd have different "pictures" for different kids with the same diagnosis, choosing the images to match the way they naturally talked about their experience. Because Alicia had likened her first experience with the intrusive thoughts to "a brick hitting me on the head," Mr. Havrilla called intrusive thoughts "bricks" whenever he spoke to her.

In order to make the neurological basis for the disease understandable, Alicia was given the imagery of there being something in the brain that acts as a vacuum cleaner. All thoughts left trails behind them, little pieces of thoughts, which had to be picked up. When you have OCD, your "vacuum cleaner" doesn't work very well, and so instead of getting picked up these little pieces of thoughts float around and combine themselves with other pieces of thoughts to make intrusive thoughts. Those intrusive thoughts in turn can't be swept away because the "vacuum cleaner" is not strong enough. Throwing more thoughts at them increases the "mess" and so makes the situation worse.

While this imagery doesn't exactly match the scientific model, it was in some ways a good "myth" or metaphor for OCD; it was easy to understand and very descriptive of what having the disorder felt like. It did help Alicia learn to Re-attribute her intrusive thoughts (or "bricks") to a neurological problem. However, it was only a child's model, and Alicia was nearly sixteen. She should have been given complete, accurate information about her disorder. Knowledge is the primary weapon against OCD; restricting her understanding was like forcing her to fight with one hand tied behind her back.

Not only that, in his zeal to provide a very simple explanation, Mr. Havrilla had inadvertently come up with one that sounded more like a child's fairy tale than actual facts. Alicia needed to know that what she was learning about her disorder was reality, not something Mr. Havrilla came up with in order to comfort her. When uncertainties beset her, and she felt condemned because of her "bad thoughts," she needed to know beyond any doubt that she was suffering from nothing more or less than a brain-based illness. Such uncertainties were still to come. In the sheltered atmosphere of Mr. Havrilla's office, Alicia was not likely to question anything he told her.

Mr. Adams was a different story. With his preference for the intellectual over the emotional, he of all people needed to have all the scientific facts about OCD and the most adult reasoning to support the treatment advised. But after giving only a childish explanation to Alicia, Mr. Havrilla provided scarcely any more information to her parents. Perhaps he over-estimated what they had already learned from

Dr. Elnicki; perhaps he thought it was not his job to counsel them. At any rate, in talking to the Adams, the main thing he did was sum up what he had told Alicia!

Perhaps it was partly because of this that Mr. Adams flatly refused to believe in intrusive thoughts. "Alicia needs to learn to think, and not be afraid of thinking. To classify a thought, just because it's an unpleasant thought, as an intrusive thought, is just…" He shook his head and wouldn't say what it was. He went on to tell Mr. Havrilla that he himself had had all kinds of thoughts and he never considered them intrusive.

Mr. Havrilla seemed completely unable to handle this. He was great with children, but Mr. Adams was too much for him. So he ducked the issue, and Mr. Adams' tragic misunderstanding of the situation went uncorrected. This left Mr. and Mrs. Adams unable to reinforce what Alicia was learning in her counseling sessions. Because they were never taught how to support their daughter, much of her battle against OCD would be fought on her own.

It would be lonely. But then, Alicia was used to being lonely.

© Copyright 2005
Alicia Adams
40 Peony Ave Apt. 14
Middletown PA 17057

Chapter Six:
One Step Forward... Two Steps Back

With the combination of medication and counseling, Alicia got better. The thoughts disappeared and her depression lifted. She began to eat and sleep normally and to enjoy life once more. And while she didn't experience any drastic personality change, she became less withdrawn than previously. She felt "herself" again, as she had in the time between the two depressions, but this second illness and the accompanying diagnosis had changed her in a way her first bout of depression had not. A new openness had arisen as she was forced to recognize her mind's vulnerability to the intrusive thoughts. She had once sought to retreat from the world around her into the refuge of her mind; now she had learned that her own brain could turn against her and could not be relied upon. She had learned a valuable lesson about retreating so far into herself, and was determined to look outward a bit, to see if she couldn't be more like other people. As her mother put it, she was finally taking notice of the world around her.

Her social skills remained very poor – she still had almost no concept of how to relate to other teenagers – but the important change was this: she knew that she did not know, and she wanted to learn. But how did one discover the secret of being normal? She watched the others at school as closely as she could, hoping to find something out. There seemed to be so much she was in ignorance of. Not just the obvious things like slang and fashions, but all the complex social behaviors that were second nature to everyone else.

Her ignorance was perhaps all the more frustrating because she liked the other girls so much. She knew that she was in a great school, the best she had ever attended. She realized that she couldn't ask for better circumstances for which to make friends. If only she knew how! She wished that someone would help her learn these things. No one seemed to understand that she really did not know how to be like the other kids. If she tried to talk about it, she was only given vague platitudes – "think of others," "to have a friend be a friend." This left her feeling more confused and threatened. What was she actually supposed to do? What was it that she was supposed to understand and did not? What was wrong with her? Often Alicia felt like there was something she was missing – as if everyone had a secret she wasn't in on.

The "secret" Alicia isn't in on is nonverbal communication – "all human responses that are not words (either spoken or written) but convey meaning, especially emotional meaning." Nonverbal signs include facial expressions, tone of voice, body language, and much more. For most people, reading and sending such messages is so natural that they are not even aware of it! For some people, however, the inability to read nonverbal signs makes even basic interactions confusing and relationships difficult. They have dyssemia – literally, "difficulty with signs."

Dr. Nowicki and Dr. Duke estimate that about ten out of a hundred people have some degree of dyssemia. One out of the ten will have a biological-neurological basis for such difficulty. The other nine were born with the normal ability to learn nonverbal communication skills, but failed to do so. Somewhere in childhood, the development of these skills went off track. For example, most dyssemics did not have a successful "best friend" or "chum" relationship between the ages of nine and twelve. "Chums," as Norwicki and Duke call them, help each other understand the social world and correct each other's nonverbal mistakes. Children that miss out on such relationships not only experience loneliness; they also miss out on an important learning experience and may fall far behind in their development of nonverbal skills – without ever realizing it.

All Alicia knows is that there is something the other kids have that she just doesn't "get." She has no idea what it is. Nor does she have any idea how to improve. Nonverbal communication so simply taken for granted. Confronted with a child or adult who lacks the required skills, most people will not provide the individual with any (verbal!) hint of what is actually expected. It is assumed, generally without much consideration, that he or she has the skills and chooses not to use them.

At best, children like Alicia are considered "very shy" and given some consideration. At worst, they are harshly criticized for their social inabilities; told that they are selfish, immature, stupid, bad, etc. They may come to believe it. They may come to believe, as Alicia did, that they have no chance of ever fitting in anywhere.

Now, however, Alicia is beginning to shake off the lie she believed for so long. She is starting to believe that there may be a chance of what she calls "normality" for her. She doesn't know how to achieve this desired state, but she is trying to learn. That is a huge step for her.

However it is all dependent upon her continuing to experience adequate mental health. Even those who are competent at social interaction can lose such abilities during a bout of depression. It would be very unusual for someone to experience a significant improvement in their social ability while depressed.

Alicia Adams

All seemed well: as winter turned to spring and spring to summer, Alicia remained completely free from both the intrusive thoughts and depression. June and July too passed with no return of the symptoms. Alicia continued to take her medication faithfully, but she was rather losing interest in her counseling appointments. With her return to health, she looked at Mr. Havrilla with a slightly more critical eye – she wasn't forgetting how good he'd been for her in her illness, but maybe she was outgrowing him now. After all, he was really for little kids, and she was sixteen.

That summer she volunteered at two preschools. One of them was for young special needs children. It was there she met five-year-old Eddie. Eddie was autistic, nonverbal, and given to frequent rages in which he would hurt himself and anyone else in his path. For such a small child he was capable of a lot of harm, and at first Alicia shied away from him, preferring the calmer children. But one day the teacher bent down to Eddie, who had been screaming all the morning, and said to him, "Poor little boy, I wish I could X-ray your head and see what the chemicals are doing." That brief interchange had a profound impact on Alicia – suddenly she almost identified with this little boy. She knew what it was to be a prisoner in one's own head, held captive to a neurological problem nobody else could see. For her it had been only for a short time; only until she got proper help. With diagnosis and treatment, she had quickly recovered. What must it be like to be forever at the mercy of one's brain chemistry – with no treatment available and not even the ability to tell somebody what was going on. And as a little child!

Alicia suddenly found herself to be very fortunate indeed. From that day on she had a new empathy for children like Eddie. She wondered if she had been permitted to experience a mental disorder so that she could feel some of what they experienced. Now that she was well again (for good, she hoped), she wanted to give something back. She wanted to teach such children someday.

It seemed like a very long time to wait until she could be of much use, however. She would have liked to help out at the preschool every day, but they only needed volunteers once a week, and sometimes not even that often. Enrollment was down a bit in the summertime. The other preschool also gave her fewer hours than she wanted, and seemed to have little for her to do when she was there. If Alicia had been a little older she might have looked for more opportunities and perhaps found a place that could have used her. However, she got no further than discussing the matter with her father, telling him how frustrating it was not to be needed. He didn't understand that she meant that she wanted to do more; he thought she was complaining of being bored, as he would have done in her place. He replied only, "Well, you don't have to volunteer at all, if you don't like it. Enjoy your summer; it'll probably the last one when you're not working."

So Alicia enjoyed her summer, enjoyed it all the more because she was conscious all the time of how wonderful her life had become now that she was well. Even after several months of good health, she had not ceased to relish being able to sleep through the night, eat normally, and amuse herself all day with her books and walks – never being bothered by the intrusive thoughts and never bothering her parents with them either. Her hopes for the future were high; she felt that the fall would be a fresh start for her. She would really try to be like the other girls, and now that she was well she just might manage it.

This delightful state of things might have lasted longer still… if not for her father's fatal combination of ignorance and arrogance. When Alicia first went on Prozac, Mr. Adams did some research on the medication, and learned that most people taking the antidepressant can go off it within a few months of the end of their depression. Unfortunately, the book he read dealt only with depression – not with OCD. Mr. Adams did not realize that the brain dysfunction that causes OCD remains even after the depression ends. He still had not fully accepted that there ever was a neurological problem, and he convinced himself that even if there had been, it must be cured by now.

He believed this so firmly that he didn't even think it was worthwhile to inform Alicia's doctor before he had her begin weaning herself off the medication. Alicia had been surprised to hear from him that it was not necessary to take Prozac for more than a few months… she had fully expected to take it for the rest of her life, like a diabetic taking insulin. However, she trusted that her father must know what he was doing, and began taking her medication every other day, just as he had told her to do.

It was a dreadful mistake. Alicia had already been on the very minimum dosage for an adolescent. Ten milligrams every other day was for all practical purposes the same as not taking medication at all. The results of this medication change were exactly what Alicia's doctor would have predicted if he'd been given the chance. Alicia's brain simply was not able to maintain its own chemical balance, and her caudate nucleus quickly became stuck. The intrusive thoughts returned, worse than before. Suddenly, Alicia became obsessed with fears that she had committed blasphemy of the Holy Spirit – the most painful obsession of all for the Christian, and one that is quite common for those with the purely obsessional form of OCD.

> *This particular obsession is so characteristic of OCD that it is among the earliest obsessions on record. "As far back as the Middle Ages," recounts Marc Summers, "church writings vividly described monks, priests, and laypeople suffering from blasphemous thoughts, demoralizing indecision, compulsive scripture reading, and pathological doubting… it was believed that these people were possessed by the devil, who besieged them with blasphemous or aggressive images. People were sometimes burned at the stake for these supposed demonic possessions."*
>
> *Later on, these symptoms began to be recognized as an illness, and termed "religious melancholy." One of the most famous sufferers of religious melancholy was William Cowper, the 18th century poet and hymnwriter*

who experienced bouts of insanity and made three attempts at suicide. There were many others:

"The Oxford Don, Robert Burton, reported a case in his compendium, the Anatomy of Melancholy (1621): 'If he be in a silent auditory, as at a sermon, he is afraid he shall speak aloud and unaware, something indecent, unfit to be said.' In 1660, Jeremy Taylor, Bishop of Down and Connor, Ireland, was referring to obsessional doubting when he wrote of "scruples": [A scruple] is trouble where the trouble is over, a doubt when doubts are resolved." In his 1691 sermon on religious melancholy, John Moore, Bishop of Norwich, England, referred to individuals obsessed by "naughty, and sometimes Blasphemous Thoughts [which] start in their Minds, while they are exercised in the Worship of God [despite] all their endeavors to stifle and suppress them ... the more they struggle with them, the more they increase."

Today this obsession accounts for perhaps five percent of all cases of OCD. Alicia's case is far from unique. Of course, she doesn't know that.

Alicia was caught completely off guard. She hadn't realized that the decrease in her medication could trigger a relapse, and even if she had she would not have imagined anything like this. In panic that consumed her, she forgot everything that Mr. Havrilla had attempted to teach her about how to deal with her intrusive thoughts. The knowledge had not truly sunk in before. The medication had worked almost too quickly; the thoughts disappeared before she had to learn how to deal with them.

Now she didn't Re-label or Re-attribute the new thoughts to her neurological problem, but considered herself condemned. But if she had forgotten Mr. Havrilla's lessons, she remembered everything else from her previous depressions – remembered them so vividly that it was like being in a time warp. It might have been an hour ago since she vomited in the car on that dreadful night she wanted to die, or since the morning her father had terrified her so much. Meanwhile, the months when she had been well seemed like nothing but a dream. She felt as if she had always been trapped in this living nightmare, and that she always would be. There was no way out.

She didn't know what to do. She was afraid to tell anyone, especially her father. She was afraid that if she went to him with the thoughts again, they would go right back into that horrible compulsive cycle in which she kept on telling him about her thoughts and he kept on getting angrier and angrier because he couldn't help her. If she had learned nothing else from her previous depression, she had learned how destructive that compulsion had been to both of them. She wanted to avoid it if she could. She reasoned that if she could resist that "need to tell, ask, or confess," then she hadn't really gone back into her illness, had she? She hoped that she could hold out until her next appointment with Mr. Havrilla. Mr. Havrilla would know how to help her. Maybe Dad would never even have to know!

But the wait was too long. The thoughts were killing her. The compulsion to tell somebody was so strong, and her father was the only one available. (Somehow she never even thought about telling her mother.) Perhaps this time would be different; perhaps this time he would help and not hurt her. Maybe, just maybe, he had changed. At the very least, he ought to be a bit more aware of her problem than he had been before.

So she approached him with a desperate hope mixed in with great fear. Her trepidation was more than justified by events. Mr. Adams took the news that she was again suffering from intrusive thoughts very badly indeed.

First he refused to believe it and accused her of lying to him. Then he angrily demanded why she hadn't told him earlier. When she tried to explain that she was trying to avoid a compulsive behavior, he had no idea what she was talking about! Although she had trusted him to tell her when she was ready to go off her medications, he actually knew far less about OCD than she did, let alone the doctors he had refused to speak to.

When she timidly tried to explain that his behavior during her previous bouts of OCD had made her fearful of involving him once more with her thoughts... he berated her for holding grudges, as if it were a sin to learn from experience. He always considered it very unchristian to remember that he had ever done anything wrong, and completely disregarded her tearful protest that she had really tried to forget.

She had tried, and had almost succeeded in repressing the memory - until the thoughts began again, and all the memories of her previous depressions came back full force. Alicia didn't want to remember such things and she didn't want to be afraid to talk to her father. She still loved him and wished things could be as they were before she ever got sick. Couldn't he see that? Did he truly have no idea of the anguish she was suffering?

Actually, he did not. Mr. Adams suffered from paranoia – or more often, those around him suffered. He would always believe that everybody was out to hurt him, to deceive him, to somehow take advantage of him. This, along with certain other characteristics, is evidence that he too has a form of OCD, though not the classic form that Alicia has. He too has an abnormal concern with harm avoidance, and a great need to defend himself against unseen dangers through the use of mental gymnastics. It was no accident that Mr. Adams' customary practice in writing or speaking was to argue against an imaginary opponent... nor was it, as he thought, merely a habit from his debate-team days. It is his version of the same mental compulsion that Alicia adopted during her depression.

For him, anything that he can not understand and explain is a huge threat. Alicia's OCD is something that doesn't fit his picture of the world – and must therefore be rejected, even if it means rejecting her too. Personal relationships had always been very difficult for him because of his constant need to protect himself from harm. He lashed out at people in response to attacks were largely imaginary. At sixteen, Alicia was just beginning to understand this, and had been very reluctant to tell him that she remembered what he had done, and worse still, had been affected by it. If she had been a little older she might not have told him at all – might have refused to answer, or come up with a nice safe lie.

Her reluctant admission put Mr. Adams on the defensive, and that meant he felt free to counter-attack. He had to defend himself against his attacker, didn't he? He told Alicia that the reason she was suffering from the thoughts again was because she was completely self-centered. She could have volunteered more that summer, he told her, forgetting that she had wanted to do just that. (What happened to 'you don't have to do it at all'?) She could have helped her mother more, but she would rather be by herself doing what she wanted to do. No wonder she had weird thoughts if so was so selfish and spent all her time alone – it was all her own fault. The merciless Mr. Adams refused to even consider the possibility that Alicia's illness was not the result of any character flaw, but the predictable result of his own decision to tinker with her medication.

Alicia was already suffering from the overwhelming guilt and fear that came with her intrusive thoughts. This cruel slander crushed her utterly. Running back to her own room, she cried and cried, wondering if it could be true. The incident was to haunt her for many years to come, years in which she would pay dearly for her father's stupid pride and his paranoid attack on her. The few weeks she was virtually without medication had completely undermined her fragile grip on mental health and sent her back to the beginning of her battle against OCD.

Worse than that – the obsession had grown since the last time. Her basal ganglia had retained the habit memories of the last time – they were all recalled by the strange "time warp" phenomenon she experienced – and she was now adding new mental compulsions as she tried more frantically than ever to ward off the "bad thoughts." Her caudate nucleus was now more "stuck" that ever before, and the extreme anxiety that her father had induced in her was the worst thing possible for that condition – even now, her "gearshift" was becoming more firmly jammed and the "wheels" spinning more out of control.

It would take much intervention even to stabilize her condition, let alone get her back to where she was just two weeks earlier. It would be four long years before she again knew a six-month respite from the disorder. By refusing to listen to the doctors, Mr. Adams had stolen four years of his daughter's youth – and he had blamed her for it.

He would never quite realize what he had done.

© Copyright 2005
Alicia Adams
40 Peony Ave Apt. 14
Middletown PA 17057

Chapter Seven: Pain

The days that followed were a blur of pain. Alicia resumed her daily medication, but there was no change in the thoughts – if anything, they were only getting worse as she exerted all her energies to suppress them. For of course, this is exactly what she should not have done! It is at this point that she really should have had somebody around who could recall to her what she has been taught about Re-labeling and Re-attributing, and keep on reminding her that she is suffering from a neurological problem – nothing else.

She had no one like that. Instead she had Mr. Adams, who continued to attack Alicia virtually every time he saw her miserable face. She just took it – his accusations, his constant mocking of her pain, his total contempt for her as a person. She had no spirit left even to attempt to defend herself. Between his condemnation and that provided by her disease, she felt unworthy of life and again began having suicidal thoughts. Furthermore she again became unable to sleep or eat, and sleep deprivation further undermined her condition.

After what seemed like eons of indescribable pain, she was able to go to her counseling appointment with Mr. Havrilla – her parents had arranged to have it moved up a bit. Alicia never told Mr. Havrilla about what her father had said to her. The subject was far too painful to speak of. Instead, she told Mr. Havrilla about the few weeks without medication and about how she had been having the most horrible thoughts and she just could not make them stop! She told him of her fear that she had committed the unforgivable sin. Mr. Adams had taken the fear as evidence of Alicia's unbelief and had been incredibly offended by it. Far be it from him to provide any comfort or reassurance to such a depraved person!

As always Mr. Havrilla was incredibly calm and showed no evidence of surprise. He explained that, in all the cases of OCD he had seen in which the obsession had "taken on a spiritual twist," it seemed inevitable for the patient to begin fearing that he or she had committed the unforgivable sin. That fear was a part of the illness; it had nothing to do with the patient's faith or lack of it. And of course there was nothing to the fear really. "If someone really committed blasphemy, it would be nothing to them. What you have is a neurological problem, Alicia – like a hiccup in the brain. These thoughts aren't coming from your soul, not from the part of you that joins with God. And he listens to your spirit and not the brain when it's hiccupping."

Mr. Havrilla probably didn't know half as much theology as Mr. Adams. But he had something that was much more important – an understanding heart, and the ability to empathize with someone in trouble. Alicia never forgot his kindness and the wisdom he showed on that occasion. In one short appointment, he joined Alicia in her fight and let her know that she was not alone. He even gave her hope. She must go back on her medication and continue her counseling appointments, and she would get better.

Alicia wished she could stay at the clinic instead of having to go back home. In the car, she stared out the window and tried not to cry. She hoped her father would not be home.

He was, though. Mrs. Adams summed up the appointment: "He told her she wasn't wicked. – just crazy."

Alicia sheepishly replied, "That's about the size of it."

"Why?" asked Mr. Adams defensively. "Because she spent the whole summer thinking of no one but herself!"

Mrs. Adams testily replied, "No, because she was without medication for all this time. I thought all along it was a bad idea to mess with it."

Mr. Adams exploded, "Excuse me for living!"

Alicia slipped up the stairs. She didn't know who she hated most, her mother or her father. Couldn't dad take any responsibility for what he'd done to her? Couldn't he apologize or admit he'd made a mistake? Couldn't he at least stop blaming her all the time? And... Mom had known all along that stopping the medication was bad for her, and she said nothing - nothing to keep this disaster from happening, and nothing to ease her pain once it had. She had never tried to stop Dad from attacking Alicia, never contradicted his harsh assessment. How much would it have meant to Alicia, to have someone even suggest that she might not be to blame for the illness that had befallen her. And Mom couldn't be bothered to provide that comfort. What kind of parents were they? Did they want to destroy her? If so, they were doing a remarkably good job of it.

School began, and Alicia was still at the peak of her illness. Her already tortured mind had received a terrible assault at the time it was most vulnerable, and the effects of that would not fade quickly. During the first few weeks of school things only got worse. Alicia tried so hard to concentrate on her work, but her brain hiccupped all day and churned out worse and worse thoughts, or so it seemed. She still wasn't sleeping well, and trying to re-adjust to the school routine further drained her energies. So much for becoming like the other girls; she felt more cut off than ever before. What right had she to even be among them? She wasn't worthy; she would contaminate them somehow. She felt herself to be a thing diseased.

Her classmates would have been astonished to learn the half of this. Outwardly, Alicia had changed little. She worked very hard at keeping herself together and appearing as normal as she could. She said little of her troubles; occasionally she would ask for prayer during Bible class, but on such occasions she was generally too overcome with emotion to be really coherent. Her teacher and classmates were tactful enough not to press her for more information, but simply prayed that she would soon feel better.

By the time of her next appointment with Mr. Havrilla, it was apparent that ten milligrams of Prozac was not enough to stabilize her and end the horrible depression that was in. Her dosage was increased to twenty a day, and at last she began to show some signs of improvement. Even then it was a slow fight, with more setbacks than Alicia would have believed possible.

Over the next two years, she was never free from the intrusive thoughts for more than a few months at a time. Stress and/or illness would trigger a relapse just when she thought she was almost well. After awhile, she became accustomed to the repeated disappointment. She was sensible enough not to waste her energies fighting against what seemed to be her fate. She considered that she had no choice but to accept her situation; she would only get worse if she blamed herself for the thoughts or kept trying to suppress them. To the best of her ability she followed Mr. Havrilla's instructions to relax and ignore the thoughts. She tried very hard not to give way to the anxiety they still produced in her, and clung as tightly as she could to any mental health that she had, any trace of "normalcy" that she find. She was determined to function as well as she could in spite of her illness. Externally, she coped so well that only Mr. Havrilla ever knew how sick she really was – if he did.

Mr. Adams, however, only grew more frustrated with the situation. Never understanding or accepting Alicia's condition, he continued to undermine her efforts to Re-label and Re-attribute. Mr. Havrilla was working so hard to teach her how to deal with the thoughts, but without support at home it wasn't as effective as it might have been. The brief appointments, every few weeks, were just enough to keep Alicia functioning. Again and again he had to keep telling her that, no matter what her father said, her illness was not her fault – it was a neurological problem that had to be treated as such if she was going to get well. Alicia had every word of his speech memorized, she could and did repeat it to herself between sessions, but she still needed to hear it from somebody else. It would have meant so much to her if her parents could have understood her OCD well enough to reassure her themselves, instead of fanning the flames of her fears. Perhaps then she and Mr. Havrilla could actually have moved forward in her therapy, instead of constantly going over the same ground. But that was not to be.

How Alicia craved some support from someone besides her counselor! She looked for it at home, and never found it. Her father was unable to accept her condition; her mother was generally unwilling to even get involved. Mrs. Adams was a very practical woman; she liked problems that had a simple and obvious solution, and preferred to avoid what she vaguely termed "deep thinking." For years, she had tolerated her husband's abstractions and tendencies to mental compulsions; she considered Alicia's illness as more of the same nuisance and didn't believe that she had either the patience or the ability to deal with it. So whenever possible she avoided discussing Alicia's illness, and when she did it was with such obvious annoyance that vulnerable Alicia felt herself to be a blot upon creation.

She looked for help at school, and sometimes had slightly better success. At least she could talk to her teachers without them getting upset or feeling offended by the existence of her illness. None of her teachers knew anything about OCD, other than the garbled account that Alicia gave them. Their ignorance didn't prevent them from being sympathetic and comforting, but on one occasion it was dangerous.

Her well-meaning Bible teacher advised her to try and replace the thoughts with Scripture. "If a thought comes into your mind and you didn't put it there, you should be able to get it out. You can't control your feelings, but you can control what you think about." It had been awhile since Alicia's last counseling appointment, and her "batteries" were running low. She didn't stop to think about what she had learned from Mr. Havrilla about the nature of OCD, but eagerly took Mr. Dukeman's advice - with disastrous results.

The more she tried to push away the thoughts and recite a Scripture verse in their place, the more her brain hiccupped. Bits of the verse would get mixed up with the intrusive thoughts, causing them to become more confused and "evil" than before. Alicia kept on trying and in the effort, became more and more pulled in. She was actually starting to disassociate from the world around her as her attention was totally focused upon her own mind. She became a complete zombie; scarcely seeing or hearing anything about her, and unable to respond. Finally a tension headache overtook her, and she was too overcome to try and fight the thoughts anymore. She came out of her trance, and dismally pronounced the effort a complete failure.

She had learned a valuable lesson, though. She could not believe all that she was told; she must test it to see if it was consistent with what she already knew about the disorder. She was finding out that most people, even adults she looked up to and trusted, didn't know anything about her illness, and in their ignorance would make unhelpful or even dangerous suggestions. She would have to be strong enough to not only stand up to the disease, but to ignore those people who would – innocently or otherwise – undermine her efforts at overcoming it.

Alicia discovered that the person who represented the greatest threat to her recovery was her father... her own father whom she had once loved so much and been so proud of. He had taught her so much and she had accepted everything he told her; she'd idolized him. But now Alicia saw her father as the devil himself, as the "Accuser" who was constantly condemning her. He had become oddly merged with her illness: the anxiety he produced in her fueled her OCD, and the OCD gave him a reason to attack her. She often wished that he had died before she got sick. If only she could have lived her life remembering him as she once thought she was instead of having to find out how cruel he could be. If only he'd never had to see her sick, maybe he'd still love her.

One of the worst episodes of that year occurred when she was in the car with him. She had come home from school after a particularly hard day with the thoughts; in fact, she had become hysterical in the afternoon and it had taken two teachers to calm her down. Alicia was feeling a little better now; the thoughts had gotten a little quieter, although she was worn out and having another tension headache. She knew better than to mention any of this to her father, and would have disappeared to her room if he had not offered to take her to rent a movie. Alicia thought that perhaps a movie would be just the thing to distract her and perhaps keep the thoughts from getting "loud" again, so she agreed.

On the way, Mr. Adams kept up a continual monologue. Alicia didn't hear a single word of it; she was concentrating on keeping calm. The comfort of her teachers had temporarily alleviated her anxiety; a few hours later, the effect was quickly wearing off. The thoughts were getting louder again, and her headache was getting progressively worse. The pain was blinding her. As much as she hated to mention it, she felt she had no choice. "Take me home, please. I have an awful headache."

Mr. Adams was more furious than Alicia had ever seen him. How dare she say that his conversation had given her a headache!

In vain, Alicia tried to explain that she had made no such accusation, that she had been sick all day and that it had nothing to do with him.

He refused to believe it. "Listening to me talk made it worse. You hate me so much. You always blame me for everything!" He continued to rant and rave all the way home. Alicia's head nearly split open and she cried and cried. Nothing she could have said would have convinced him that she had meant no personal attack, and now she could not speak at all.

That was the worst day, but there were many that were little better. Slowly, slowly, that year went by, marked chiefly by Alicia's frequent relapses into OCD and depression. The strangest things could trigger them. For instance, an unfortunate incident occurred at school: somebody stole a little kid's Bible and wrote obscenities in it. Alicia didn't see it, but she and her classmates were told that the person had written "blasphemous" things. That set Alicia off again, thinking about her own bad thoughts. She'd just recently recovered from a bad spell, and it didn't take much to trigger a relapse. She felt as guilty as if she had been the one who committed the vandalism.

"Alicia," asked Mr. Havrilla, "when you hear that someone else has done wrong, do you kind of personalize it? Do you think, 'I might do that?'"

Alicia nodded. "But it's even worse than that sometimes – I feel as if I really had done the thing."

Mr. Havrilla nodded, and told her that it wasn't all that uncommon for people with OCD to have oversensitive consciences. One man he knew felt guilty because he overheard a co-worker talking about an affair. Alicia had to keep remembering that the bad feelings were just a part of the illness, and not take them seriously. "You know you didn't have anything to do with the vandalism. It's hard for you, I know, because you are so used to drawing comfort from your school. You feel like your refuge has been invaded. But this is something that will all blow over soon."

It did, but as usual the reprieve was short-lived.

It was spring, and Alicia seemed to be getting worse again. Both Mr. and Mrs. Adams ran out of patience. They didn't understand why their daughter never seemed to get better and alternated between blaming her and blaming her doctors. They didn't appreciate Mr. Havrilla's efforts with their daughter and never thought to try and continue that work at home. Instead, they were considering "starting over," looking for a new diagnosis and new treatment.

Alicia was horrified that they would even consider interfering with her treatment again. She hadn't even recovered from their last mistake yet! She tried to tell them.

"I need Mr. Havrilla."

"What does Mr. Havrilla do other than smile?" asked Mrs. Adams. Usually Mrs. Adams was completely passive toward Alicia's illness, but this time she had taken Mr. Adams' side against her.

"He talks to me… he explains that it's a neurological problem and that it's not my fault."

"And you want him to say that one more time?" Mrs. Adams simply couldn't grasp it.

"Yes! I need it!" Alicia was in tears. Why couldn't they understand? What Mr. Havrilla was doing with her might be simple or repetitive, but it was all that kept her going sometimes. She didn't know why her medication would suddenly stop working and the thoughts would return. She hated it more than anybody else, and she hated the reaction it got from her parents. That was why she tried not to let them know when she was having a relapse. There were many days when Alicia suffered in complete silence, without a single soul to support her. But when it got really bad she couldn't hide it because she cried all the time and threw up.

"Mr. Havrilla knows my history. If I went to a stranger, I'd have to start at the very beginning of the thoughts."

"You could just tell him about this last little bit."

"That isn't the way it's done. I can't start over with a new doctor now!" Couldn't they understand that it wasn't like fixing a car or straightening teeth? Her intrusive thought pattern had a definite history to it.

"Why?" challenged Mr. Adams. "You afraid he'll tell you something you don't want to hear?" He continued to cherish the belief that Alicia's "selfishness" was responsible for her disease, and hoped that he could find someone else to agree with him. Alicia was terrified that he'd shop around until he did – someone who was completely ignorant of OCD, but would tell her father what HE wanted to hear.

She was wise enough now not to answer her father's direct attack; she knew that he would only twist her words against her. She carefully stuck to her original point, "I need to see my own counselor. Do you know how hard it is to counsel yourself?" At that time, she was working as hard as she possibly could to Re-label and Re-attribute. She got no support in this from anyone but Mr. Havrilla – just the reverse.

"About as hard as diagnosing yourself and picking the counselor," sneered Mr. Adams, and wouldn't talk to her anymore.

"Diagnosing myself!" thought Alicia, as she was consumed with all the words she would never be able to say to her cruel father. "I've seen three doctors who have all made the same diagnosis. And Dr. Elnicki picked the counselor. You're the one who wants to shop around for one that suits YOU. I wouldn't have gotten this sick in the first place if you had listened to Dr. Elnicki and not messed with my medication. And now you're just going to screw me up more and more."

The next day Alicia vented to her favorite teacher Mrs. Ludwig, "My parents don't care how much I suffer; they only pity themselves for having a crazy kid. They think I should have "outgrown" my neurological problem by now. No one would like that better than me, but it's not in my control. And now they're threatening to take away my medication. It'll be like the days before the diagnosis – I won't be able to sleep or eat or concentrate on anything. No, this time it'll be worse; my problem has grown since THEY played with my medicine before." Even to Mrs. Ludwig she could not voice all her fears: "I'll probably end up in a mental institution. Or I'll kill myself. I was close to being suicidal before, and I'd rather die than get any sicker than I already am."

Alicia's fears may be exaggerated, but not entirely unfounded. Interrupting her treatment – depriving her of both the medication and the counseling that she needs – would have been an incredibly dangerous and foolish thing to do. Especially if Mr. Adams set out to find some quack that would promise a quick solution and not bother him with the medical facts he didn't want to accept. Alicia's best interest isn't being even being considered; Mr. and Mrs. Adams are only acting out their own frustrations and their own needs.

This situation is far from unique. No one knows how many children suffer torments everyday because of their parents' refusal to accept their mental illness or disability. Denial – and the willful ignorance that it leads to – is one of the most dangerous things on earth.

In the end, Mr. and Mrs. Adams didn't look for a new counselor. They let things go on the way they were. They never said why, and Alicia asked no questions. She felt as if she'd been granted a stay of execution. It was not something she wanted to tamper with.

© Copyright 2005
Alicia Adams
40 Peony Ave Apt. 14
Middletown PA 17057

Chapter Eight: A Hidden Disability

That spring, Alicia's medication was increased to 30 milligrams a day. Dr. Elnicki explained that such increases in medication were often necessary in response to increased stress on the patient. He did not, however, question Alicia to find out where this increased stress might be coming from. He thought he already knew. "Senior-itis," he pronounced. "I've got a daughter just her age, and I know the pressures these kids are under – looking at colleges and trying to figure out what they'll do with their lives."

Later on at home, Mrs. Adams said that it was the first time Dr. Elnicki had acted like a human being instead of a machine. He'd actually turned around in his chair to look at them, and had been so genial in talking about his daughter and about teens growing up. It had actually been a pleasant visit.

Alicia too had enjoyed the new-and-improved Dr. Elnicki, and she was somewhat gratified to have someone recognize that she'd been under a lot of pressure. Her father never understood that. He was always talking about how lazy she was. Just a few months ago, she had been unfortunate enough to have an attack of OCD just before midterms. She tried to keep up her studying just the same, but the illness left her so drained that she once feel asleep over her chemistry book, only to wake to her father's voice: "Alicia's allergic to work!" Even the A's and B's she earned on the exams did not remove the sting of that assessment. It was so unfair. Even when she worked her hardest, she was called lazy.

No one who has not experienced OCD can fully understand just how exhausting it is. The hyperactivity in the brain takes up much energy. So do the compulsions or the resistance of the compulsions. Sleep disturbances also take their toll. Taken together, it is not surprising that Alicia's stamina would be low, and her need for rest high. But Mr. Adams never understood that. Just when Alicia most needed to relax, he pushed her harder than ever – and not only about schoolwork. Somewhere along the way he had gotten the unshakeable idea that "downtime" was not good for Alicia's condition, that it lead to an increase in the thoughts. So he tried to keep her busy. No doctor had ever suggested anything remotely like this, and Alicia had tried and tried to tell him that being rushed and pressured was in fact a major trigger for her thoughts, but he would not listen. He was still convinced that he knew more about her illness than anyone else – more than the doctors who had studied it all their lives, more than someone who was actually living with the disorder for the second year in a row. And this without bothering to read anything about the disorder or ask Alicia what it was like to have it. His arrogance was truly an amazing thing.

Mrs. Adams was no help, either. When Alicia told her that the thoughts had come back, she demanded, "When are you finding time to think them?" Alicia tried to explain that it wasn't a matter of time, that the thoughts went on no matter what she was doing, like a headache or a fever. She woke up in the morning to find them already going through her head, and they continued as long as she was awake. Yet her parents thought they could keep her busy enough to eliminate them! In the year since her diagnosis, they had learned nothing.

So Alicia felt a bit vindicated by Dr. Elnicki's recognition of the stress in her life. However, he had been a little hasty in his diagnosis of the cause. "Senior-itis" was hardly Alicia's problem. Graduation from high school wasn't even on her radar screen yet. College and the future barely merited a thought. Nearly a year ago she had resolved to become a special education teacher "someday," but she had no plan for reaching that distant goal. She was operating in survival mode, battling her illness one day at a time. The disease was the focal point of her existence.

This was incomprehensible to her parents, particularly Mrs. Adams, who wanted to sympathize with her daughter and did not know how. If Alicia confided that she was "having a bad day," Mrs. Adams was eager to find some concrete cause for it. Did someone at school say something mean, or did they ignore her? Did she get a bad grade, or did she have a headache? These were things Mrs. Adams could understand. The thoughts were outside her experience. She was equally baffled by Alicia's delight in a "good day," which did not depend on any attention from other kids or any recognizable event, but on the shift in her brain chemistry. To Mrs. Adams this was not only perplexing but offensive. Why did Alicia have to be so difficult? What a self-centered child, ignoring the rest of the world to concentrate on her bizarre thoughts. Just like her father. She might not be able to do anything about him, but she wasn't about to encourage her daughter in such foolishness.

And so the wedge between Alicia and her parents deepened. They resented her illness and felt that they'd been cheated of the child they were supposed to have. Mrs. Adams, in particular, was keenly aware of the differences between Alicia and her peers. Why couldn't Alicia take an interest in clothes and boys, like other girls? Why didn't she ever go do things with her friends? Why did she have to be so weird? Confronted with Alicia's differences, Mrs. Adams often felt like a failure as a mother, and she worried about what would happen to Alicia once she went off to college. How would she ever manage to get along with a roommate? Would she be able to take care of herself? What if she continued to have this… whatever…. called OCD?

Up until now Mrs. Adams had wanted to stay out of it, hoping that Alicia would outgrow her "thoughts." But now she began to be more interested in Alicia's counseling appointments. She felt that Mr. Havrilla needed to be pushed to actually do something for Alicia; she could see no purpose in continually repeating to Alicia that she was not responsible for the thoughts. Maybe, thought Mrs. Adams, it was about time they moved past those thoughts and onto something real. Something that made sense!

Mr. Havrilla wanted to honor Mr. and Mrs. Adams' concerns about their daughter; from the beginning he had tried to reach out to them, for his hands were tied as long as they did not support Alicia's treatment. However, he could not pretend to agree with Mr. Adams' misconceptions about her disorder, and so he had no credibility in the proud man's eyes. Mr. Havrilla knew by now that he had no chance of getting through Mr. Adams, yet he still had hopes of being able to work with Alicia's mother.

Yet there were difficulties there too. Mr. Havrilla was trained to treat OCD, but Mrs. Adams wasn't interested in that. She was much more concerned about other problems that Alicia had – her social skill deficits, her general immaturity and inability to care for herself, her lack of organization and problem-solving ability, and some difficulties with information-processing that Mrs. Adams could not really identify, but wanted someone to take notice of. Yet Mr. Havrilla couldn't see what Mrs. Adams was so worried about. In his office, Alicia really didn't seem that unusual for an OCD patient. Her thoughts and compulsions were identical to those of patients he'd had in the past, before he'd begun his work with children. As for the day-to-day difficulties that Alicia's mother worried about, he never saw them and might not have known what to make of them if he had. His training had not included a disorder that often accompanies OCD: NLD, or nonverbal learning disability.

Nonverbal learning disability (NLD) is a little understood condition; it's not surprising that no one in Alicia's world has it on their radar screen as a possibility. For NLD frequently goes undiagnosed, or is diagnosed only after a long search and several blind alleys. NLD is the opposite of what it sounds like: the person is not nonverbal; rather, he or she has difficulty processing nonverbal information, just as people with the more common language-based learning disabilities have difficulty processing verbal information.

For Alicia, dyssemia – difficulty with nonverbal communication – is the most significant part of her NLD. Other teens quickly and effortlessly decode social cues, such as tone of voice and facial expression. Because Alicia can not do this, she misses the majority of communication – many estimate nonverbal information to be about two-thirds of a typical message.

For example, she can't reliably recognize when someone is playfully teasing, when they are making fun of her, and when they are making a straightforward comment. Since this is pure guesswork for her, she's sometimes oversensitive (reading hostile intentions where they do not exist) and other times oblivious to how she is being mocked. She can't be totally sure that the people she thinks are her friends aren't making capital of her in some way, and she can't stand up for herself when is made fun of because she can't be totally sure that she is not imagining the whole thing. This is a vulnerable position to be in, and makes her insecure and unsure of herself in almost any social situation, but especially a novel or unstructured one. Because she is hesitant, she prefers to stay on the sidelines, watching and listening. She is pleased if anyone notices her and tries to draw her into a conversation, yet she doesn't need this to enjoy being with people.

This type of remoteness is very common in people with NLD, yet is open to misinterpretation. Alicia has often been condemned as being uninterested in people, as not caring about anybody else. That isn't true; she has no intention of being unfriendly. She simply doesn't have the means to join the crowd, and she feels the lack of ability. Yet whenever she tries to talk about it, she is told that she's only making excuses and that if she really wanted to join in, she could. It's the same message Alicia received from her elementary school teacher: that her isolation is her own fault, that she's just not good enough to have any friends.

This is the same destructive message that hundreds of NLD kids get every day. Since the ability to understand and respond to social cues is taken for granted, the struggles of these children are completely overlooked. Parents and teachers alike assume that the child is capable of interacting and is deliberately refusing to. The child may know this is not true, but is unable to defend himself or herself against the accusation. Any attempt to do so is ignored. Frustration mounts. The child may blame himself or herself, internalizing all the negative messages, or he or she may react with an overwhelming rage at the injustice of adults. It is not surprising that many children with NLD experience loss of self-esteem and present behavior problems. Many suffer acute depression, and may consider suicide, even at a very young age. They feel hopelessly flawed, constantly judged, and yet have not the slightest notion of what is really the matter or how to improve. Everyone seems to be against them, and they don't know why. Everything they do seems to turn out wrong, and they don't know why.

While these social skills deficits are the most heart-wrenching, there are other components to Alicia's NLD. She also has great difficulty with visual-spatial skills. In fact, she was often totally unaware of visual-spatial information. Although a good student, she found geometry to be entirely meaningless. She was halfway through the book when she casually commented, "I don't know why they put the picture next to the question every time." Upon questioning, it was revealed that she didn't realize that the diagrams in her textbook were not merely an illustration, but a source of information. Alicia was working through the geometry problems by imitating the examples given at the beginning of a lesson: she would find a "matching question" and carefully copy it, changing letters as necessary to fit the problem posed to her. She was able to do this with a high degree of accuracy, but she never understood any of the concepts involved or had any sense of the logic behind the examples. Nor did she realize that there was another way of approaching geometry.

More serious difficulties emerged as she began to drive. The concept of "reverse" baffled her, as she could not visualize where the car would go or which direction she should turn the steering wheel to get her wheels in the proper position. Parallel-parking was incomprehensible. Even in plain driving, she often failed to see other cars that were quite close. And she got lost all the time, even in very familiar places. Disorientation is a common experience for those with NLD; a place one's been to a hundred times can seem completely unfamiliar because the visual memory is not stable. Certainly visual sequencing is not stable; for example, Alicia was never certain of the order of certain landmarks she passed on the way to school, and therefore couldn't judge what she was supposed to see next. It was difficult to even know for sure if she'd taken a wrong turn.

Essentially, she did not perceive the journey from one place to another as a whole, but rather as bewildering collage of images. Maps that showed "the whole picture" of a route (her mother drew her many such) were of limited help as Alicia couldn't grasp the spatial relationships between different places, or the relationship between the map and the actual road. She did not think of a particular intersection as being related to other landmarks, but as a distinct experience. For her, learning a new route was like learning a new alphabet letter by letter. A child learning the alphabet looks at the symbol "A" and memorizes its name. Alicia looked at an intersection and memorized a direction, "Turn right here." And to her, going to a place and coming home were totally different routes; it was a real stretch for her to turn her memorized directions around, especially as the same place might not be recognizable from a different perspective.

Alicia's poor visual-spatial sense was also evident in gym class at school. She couldn't understand how the games *worked. They inevitably involved keeping track of the relative locations of a large number of people and of a ball – difficult in itself and made more complex by a myriad of rules. Alicia couldn't work out where she was supposed to stand, what she was supposed to do, or how the game could be won or lost. By this time, several of her classmates had realized her difficulty, and were now careful to direct her in any game (and to keep the ball away from her if possible). She could follow very specific directions: she went left or right as she was told to do, swung the tennis racket as instructed, ran in the same directions her teammates did. The reason for any of this was wholly obscure. Geometry, maps, and sports were all meaningless. To have NLD is to be unable to see the forest for the trees, or to even realize that there is a forest. It is to be lost in a fog of unprocessed nonverbal information. Usually, it is to be overlooked.*

Mrs. Adams tried in vain to explain what she had observed of Alicia's difficulties to Mr. Havrilla, and suggested that the girl be tested, as she might have some kind of learning disability. Mr. Havrilla was confused; he didn't know very much about learning disabilities, but like most people, he thought only in terms of the language-based learning problems that were diagnosed in school. He couldn't understand why Mrs. Adams would suspect anything like that in Alicia's case: there was no difficulty with schoolwork.

Many children with NLD are great students, especially in the early years. They're great readers and spellers; they easily remember verbal information like multiplication

> tables and social studies facts. Motor skill issues may trip them up, however: many NLD students have such difficulty writing legibly that they are unable to complete many school assignments. Alicia doesn't have that problem, so she is even more invisible than most. Since learning disabilities are primarily associated with academic difficulties, it seems impossible that a child who generally does well in school might have a learning disability that affects her functioning in non-academic areas. Yet this does happen.

Mr. Havrilla dismissed the idea of a learning disability. Yet he welcomed the idea of testing: not testing for learning disabilities, but for psychological disorders. He agreed that it was time to focus on Alicia's total development, rather than just her mental illness. Perhaps he had been remiss in not paying more attention to this area before. He arranged for Alicia to take the Minnesota Multiphasic Personality Inventory, or MMPI.

> The MMPI was designed to assist clinical psychologists to diagnose certain psychological disorders such as depression and schizophrenia by measuring different traits, such as paranoia or introversion, and determining whether the patient falls within normal limits for each. The person taking the MMPI is given a lengthy true-false test of over 500 items, most of them fairly simple statements such as "I like mechanics magazines." The test yields scores on 14 different subscales to gauge the varied aspects of personality. For example, answers to questions about gender roles or gender-related interests yield a score on the masculinity/

femininity subscale, while answers to questions about moods or outlook will yield a score on the depression subscale.

This test has been a staple of psychological practice since the 1940s: it is simple to administer and to score. Yet interpreting the results is difficult. It is not a matter of looking at a score on the depression subscale and diagnosing "depression," or looking at a score on the hysteria subscale and diagnosing "hysteria." Rather, the scores need to be examined as a group; a specific profile of scores indicates particular areas of difficulty that might be explored further. For example, a depressed "subject" might have high scores in the areas of hypochondria, depression, and hysteria; a schizophrenic "subject" would be more likely to have high scores in the areas of paranoia, schizophrenia, and social introversion.

Alicia found the test itself interesting; she was amazed at the variety of questions asked. Yet the results were not very enlightening. It was somewhat reassuring that no new psychological disorders were revealed, but other than that, Alicia and her mother were no better informed than before. Certainly they were no closer to gaining an understanding of the processing problems that hampered Alicia's social functioning; the MMPI did not address those at all. Mrs. Adams' concerns about her daughter went ignored. And Alicia would not discover her NLD for many years, and it would not be in the context of counseling…

But that is another story.

© Copyright 2005
Alicia Adams
40 Peony Ave Apt. 14
Middletown PA 17057

Chapter Nine: A Friend

How powerful childhood lessons can be! Six years had gone by since Miss Gardiner bribed the other children to be kind to Alicia. Six years in which she had never fully trusted anyone's motivations for befriending her. It was not that she did not trust the other girls in her class: they had been unfailingly kind to her since the day she transferred to the school, and had really tried to include her. She could not possibly fault them for any of their actions; indeed, she could not fault them at all. She thought they were all remarkably kind and good.

That was just the trouble. She thought that their kindness to her was a "Good Deed." Somewhere in the back of her mind, she was always haunted by the fear that they did not really like her; that they were just "being nice," doing a "kindness" to the girl who was "different," who didn't really belong. And while one can be grateful for having a good deed done to one (and Alicia was certainly very grateful), somehow "Good Deeds" don't excite any real intimacy.

In all probability, the other girls at Alicia's school would have been shocked to learn how Alicia perceived their attentions to her. They certainly never gave her any reason to believe that she was some "pet project" of theirs, or that she was in anyway unacceptable to them. Alicia didn't need reasons. In her mind, it was self-evident that she was an outsider.

If any confirmation of that fact was required, her illness (and the reaction it had drawn from her parents) were all that was necessary. After all, who could possibly want to be friends with such a freak? Actually, the other girls knew very little about what was really going on. Occasionally, she had referred to her "neurological problem" – she never used the term "OCD" or "mental illness" - either in a prayer request or in a brief explanation of why she'd left school early for an appointment. They had all been kind enough not to press for details. Alicia mentally gave them credit for another good deed.

Just when it seemed that nothing could ever change… she met Rhys. He was new in school that year. So new that he didn't know Alicia's reputation for silence; he didn't know that she had "a neurological problem" and was often "sick." Likewise, she didn't know that he'd been considered a "problem student" and a "rebel" at his former school. High school teachers are fond of telling students that a new school year is a chance to start with a clean slate, even when this is manifestly not the case as neither students nor staff have developed amnesia over the summer months. But on this occasion, it was undoubtedly true.

The really extraordinary thing about Alicia and Rhys, however, was not what they didn't know about each other. What was extraordinary was that Alicia knew that he liked her – knew it almost from the very beginning. She never once wondered if he was just being kind. The idea would never have entered her head. For the first time in a very long time, Alicia could accept that somebody really cared for her.

Alicia was very young for her age, so young that she never thought to wonder if he "liked her as a girl" or anything like that. She certainly never expected him to call her or ask her out, and so was not hurt when he did not do so. It was enough that he was happy to see her every school day – that his face lit up at the sight of her, as if he'd only been waiting for them to have a class together. It was enough that he talked to her and joked with her every day.

They were always laughing together; Rhys was so playful and full of jokes that Alicia, whose sense of humor had long been overshadowed by her illness, couldn't help but respond in kind. Within weeks, they had "their" jokes and amused their friends with their lively banter – though no one was as delighted as they were themselves. Within a few months, they were dubbed "the hilarious pair." Alicia secretly savored the epithet both for its compliment to her humor – a quality taken seriously in high school – and because it linked her so with Rhys. He was growing more and more important to her. She could hardly wait to see him each day; he was such a comfort to her. He could make her laugh on days when few people could have gotten her to smile. It wasn't just that he was able to amuse her; it was that he wanted to. He seemed to be always scanning her face to see what effect he was having, always trying to get and keep her attention. He seemed to know exactly when she most needed him to clown around and take her mind off her troubles.

For it could have been a very difficult year for her. Alicia caught a cold in early December that hung on through March, or if that is a medical impossibility, she caught several colds in quick succession during those four months. She was never very sick, but she coughed a great deal, and very loudly, much to the annoyance of her family. Worse - from Alicia's point of view – her intrusive thoughts, that had been under such good control in the summer and fall, returned. She had noticed the year before that the thoughts got worse when she had a cold, and often would not return to pre-cold levels until she'd been well a week. This winter, there was little or no time when she was perfectly well. Her intrusive thought increased and decreased along with her coughs. When both were at a peak, she didn't get much sleep.

However, Alicia was better able to cope with the thoughts that formerly. Mr. Havrilla's lessons were sinking in, and she was able to take a more objective approach to her illness. It helped that the link between her overall health and her neurological health was now so obvious; there was less temptation to spiritualize her condition or think that she was a terrible person because she couldn't control her thoughts. Rather, she was learning to regard the obsessions in the same way she did the cough… as something that was troublesome now, but would eventually pass. Over the years – and it was three years now since the first symptoms appeared – she had developed an unusual degree of patience. Now she was learning to not only endure the pain of the thoughts but to rise above them. She was not only going to survive, she was going to live!

The thoughts were background noise from an annoying radio; she couldn't stop hearing them, but she could stop listening. She was going to have a normal life in spite of them. This determination filled her up and kept her from sinking into depression as she had done in the past. There were days and weeks when she was dangerously close to sinking again. She tried to conceal those times; rarely did her family know about them.

Rhys was her best support. Not that he actually knew what was going on. Alicia did not want him to know about the OCD. A more secure person might have wanted him to know, to be able to empathize. Yet always in the back of her mind, and often at the front of it too, was the conviction if he knew about her illness he would never see her as a real person again. She would become an object of pity or curiosity, at best. After all, her illness had already come between her and her own parents. If they could not accept it, why should anyone else be expected to? No, Rhys must continue to see her as normal. With him, she felt as if she really was.

He was changing the way she felt about herself, and he was changing the way others saw her. The transformation in Alicia could not be missed by those who had known her in previous years. The nearly silent girl had found her voice, and the other girls, who had been so patient with her always, were delighted. Alicia had not only made a friend, but she was beginning to realize how many friends she had had all along – if only she had been able to recognize them as such.

At long last, she was getting a taste of what her high school experience should have been. She did not mourn for what had been lost, though; she was still so young that the present far outweighed the past and the future. Yet she knew that this could not last. It was her senior year of high school, and very soon she would be uprooted from the school she loved, the school she had once credited with pulling her out of her first depression and now honored for supporting her all through the subsequent ones. It would be time for college.

Alicia Adams

Alicia wanted to go to college, and not just because she loved to learn and hoped to have a career. Normal 18-year-olds went away to college; they were adults. And "normal" was just what Alicia wanted to be, just what she was secretly afraid she could not be. She knew that choosing the right school was important, but she really didn't know what she should be looking for. There was no one she could really talk to about it. Her parents seemed to have no idea of what it meant to find a school that would be prepared for her; instead, they talked about her defects and how unlikely it was that she would be successful in college – sometimes jokingly, sometimes worriedly, but never optimistically. Mr. Havrilla, her most trusted guide, was out of his depth here. He had never had to prepare a counselee for college before.

With no one to advise her regarding how her OCD and other challenges would affect her transition to college, Alicia did her best to figure things out on her own. After much reflection, she decided that it was most important to find a place that was a lot like her high school so she wouldn't have to deal with too many changes. She was intimidated by the reports she had heard about the dorm and social life at some colleges, including Christian colleges – in other words, she'd heard about how wild some campuses were and did not feel that she was she was prepared to deal with that type of social challenge. She wanted to continue to live in the warm cocoon that her high school had been. Where could she find a college that would offer that same shelter?

A magazine of Christian colleges seemed to provide the answer. It described a school in California known as "GMB." According to the magazine, GMB had the best teacher training program in the country, and that it also provided a very secure Christian environment. Alicia had heard of this school before and knew that it was doctrinally and culturally similar to her high school. She had heard that it was "strict," but she'd always been such a "good girl" that she feared nothing from a strict college. And she did want a good teacher training school! Alicia was very young and too quickly accepted the assessment of the magazine. She did not ask what criteria were used to determine the best teacher training program, and it is possible she would not have understood the explanation had it been given.

She went for a college visit and liked the school. The GMB campus was very beautiful and it did remind her rather of her high school. Even some of the textbooks were the same. She knew that there would be many changes and difficult adjustments regardless of where she went, but she did feel that this was the best match she was likely to find.

She never considered that the most important thing for her to look for in a college was its attitude toward mental illness. Although she had already suffered from ignorance and prejudice, she had an idea of "colleges" that was rather unrealistic; she thought that there were sure to be some better-informed people there. She was wrong. Ironically, in her efforts to find a school that would be the least stressful, Alicia actually picked out the very worst one possible for her.

Not that this was apparent at first. To a prospective student, GMB would not reveal its real attitude toward those with mental illness. When routine questions about medical history revealed Alicia's disease, the admissions department asked only she have psychological testing to determine whether she was really stable enough for college. Alicia and her parents were pleased with the idea. Although she had been tested a year before, with no apparent results, her mother still held out hope that someone would be able to give them some answers and dutifully filled out her share of the forms.

For much information had to be gathered before the actual appointment with the psychiatrist. There was a parent questionnaire which set Mrs. Adams to looking through Alicia's baby book to determine the precise ages at which she had hit certain developmental milestones. There was also a teacher questionnaire which, after some deliberation, Alicia gave to Mrs. Ludwig with a brief explanation.

Alicia took all these proceedings very seriously. At seventeen, it did not occur to her to doubt that her entire future hung upon the decision of this new doctor. When the day came that she was to leave school a few hours early and go to her appointment, she was so full of excitement and apprehension that she could resist confiding in her homeroom teacher, Mrs. Ludwig. As the school day had not yet begun, there were very few other students around – just one or two who were not, in Alicia's opinion, at all likely to repeat what they heard to Rhys. Alicia had every hope that the real nature of her appointment that day could be concealed from him.

All went well up until that afternoon. She and Rhys were in history class, chattering away as usual, when the announcement came over the loudspeaker: "Alicia Adams, your father is here to take you to your appointment." Alicia wished that the floor would open up and swallow her, although the announcement had actually revealed nothing about her mental health. (For all her classmates knew, she could have been going to the dentist.) It was the shock and horror on her face that told Rhys that something there was something significant about this appointment. Just in case further evidence was required, a girl from her first period class obligingly called out, "Goodbye, Alicia! I hope everything goes okay!"

"Where are you going?" Rhys asked, as Alicia began to gather up her books and helplessly make for the door. She could not answer him, and he asked again, louder and more insistently, "Alicia! Where are you going?" Everybody in the room was staring at them now. Alicia was halfway to the door by then, but stopped and turned around. She felt she must answer Rhys, that he deserved some kind of explanation… but she couldn't think of one. So after staring helplessly at him for several seconds, she turned again and fled. She was utterly humiliated and convinced that she had just lost her first and best friend. He would surely find out everything by the next day. All through that afternoon, she kept seeing his confused and worried face: so different from his usual expression.

In this gloomy frame of mind she went off to her evaluation. It was rather different from what she expected. The psychologist, Dr. Majithia, never actually gave her any tests. She spent the majority of the time talking to Mr. Adams, while Alicia waited outside. She spoke to Alicia only briefly.

Alicia had had very little experience talking to strange adults about her OCD. She had had the same counselor ever since she was diagnosed, two years earlier. In many ways the consistency had been a blessing; however, there were also disadvantages. Mr. Havrilla, so accustomed to children, had never been able to break the habit of talking to Alicia as if she were a young child rather than almost eighteen.

As young people with mental illnesses and/or other disabilities approach adulthood, it is vital for them to learn to self-advocate. As they assume more responsibility for their lives, they will be required to interact with many people who do not understand their problems or needs. Parents, teachers, and therapists will not always be around to offer explanations for them or to insist that they are treated fairly. The adolescent must learn to articulate the nature of his or her illness or disability and explain its effects; also to identify what supports or accommodations will be needed to succeed in a new situation. Alicia had not been taught to do any of this.

Rather than an adult explanation of her illness, Alicia had been given the imagery of there being something in the brain that acts as a vacuum cleaner: all thoughts left trails behind them, little pieces of thoughts, which had to be picked up. According to this model, when you have OCD, your "vacuum cleaner" doesn't work very well, and so instead of getting picked up these little pieces of thoughts float around and combine themselves with other pieces of thoughts to make intrusive thoughts. Those intrusive thoughts in turn can't be swept away because the "vacuum cleaner" is not strong enough. Throwing more thoughts at them increases the "mess" and so makes the situation worse.

She stumbled through this explanation, which was made more difficult by the fact that English was not Dr. Majithia's primary language, and also by Alicia's determination not to actually say her "bad thoughts" aloud. In spite of Mr. Havrilla's efforts, she still felt ashamed of the thoughts that so often intruded into her mind. She had accepted the fact that she could not control them, but still she wanted to keep them hidden.

Dr. Majithia soon gave up trying to get a clearer explanation from Alicia. She started asking instead about her friendships. It could not be a more unfortunate time for asking about that. Alicia felt she'd just lost her only chance of ever having a normal friend. She could not bring herself to talk of Rhys. All that was over. When she returned to school the next day she would be returning to the loneliness that was her fate.

And so the account Dr. Majithia received of Alicia's social life was not an account of the previous six months. It was a rather bitter reflection of her situation as it had been in other years. "I never fit in at school. The other girls are nice to me, but I don't know how to respond." All Dr. Majithia's questions were answered in a similarly dispirited fashion. Alicia was representing her social abilities in the worst possible light. Perhaps Dr. Majithia can not be blamed for the conclusions she was drawing, as she asked another question: how was she with change?

"Terrible," replied Alicia. "Any stress tends to bring on more intrusive thoughts."

At this point Dr. Majithia was not surprised. Mr. Adams had presented an even bleaker picture. He of course knew nothing of Rhys or the girl that Alicia had become in the last six months. He hadn't actually seen her try to interact with other kids for about a year. He took for granted that nothing had changed. His own opinions unfortunately had not altered very much in the past two years since Alicia had been diagnosed with OCD. He still believed that she really didn't care about anyone else. He had anticipated her judgment on her ability to handle change; not taking into account, any more than she did, the vulnerability caused by her illness.

It was primarily on these two interviews that Dr. Majithia formed her conclusions; the questionnaires did little to counter the impression that had been made. Perhaps she took Alicia and Mr. Adams too much at face value: she could not have known that Alicia was not exactly her usual self on that afternoon, or that Mr. Adams' perceptions of the situation were questionable due to his own personal problems. Then again, maybe it wouldn't have made any difference if Alicia had been at her best, or if Mr. Adams had been more aware of his daughters' progress in developing social skills.

Dr. Majithia delivered a stunning verdict: Alicia had Asperger's Syndrome, a form of autism. Social inability, great difficulty with change, poor communication ability along with high intelligence: it was a fairly typical profile for an "Asperger's kid." Her way of broaching the subject was perhaps unnecessarily cruel. "Remember the movie *Rain Man*?"

Asperger's syndrome and autism have been defined by the American Psychiatry Academy as pervasive developmental disorders, characterized by extreme difficulty with communication and socialization. Asperger's syndrome is sometimes confused with high-functioning autism; yet there is a distinction between the two. Autistic individuals typically have problems with both verbal and nonverbal communication and also exhibit unusual behaviors such as hand flapping or echolalia; often their visual-spatial abilities far exceed their verbal skills. People with Asperger's, however, generally have relatively good verbal language yet can't master nonverbal communication or understand social situations; they have a restricted range of interests and restricted relationships with others. With either diagnosis, there is an extremely wide range of severity. Some people with Aspergers' have extreme social and behavioral difficulties and can be easily recognized as "odd." But many others have quite subtle challenges that are not readily noticed.

Alicia does have characteristics of Asperger's, as do many people with nonverbal learning disabilities. In fact, some professionals have questioned whether there is any real difference between Asperger's and NLD, as the two so often overlap. Dr. David Dinklage writes, "It is possible that the symptoms of each diagnosis describe the same group of children from different perspectives, AD from either a psychiatric/behavioral perspective, and NVLD from a neuropsychological perspective. The specific conventions of these diagnoses may lead to a somewhat different group of children meeting diagnostic criteria."

Basically, NLD is a cognitive profile consisting of high verbal comprehension and low perceptual organization or

> *nonverbal skills. This cognitive profile can be revealed by a neuropsychological evaluation given by a psychologist. Asperger's, however, is a psychiatric diagnosis made by a psychiatrist on the basis of certain behavioral characteristics. Although the two are diagnosed very differently, most people with Asperger's also meet the criteria for NLD and many professionals suspect that the reverse is also true.*

Dr. Majithia said that Alicia should begin group therapy with other teens that had Asperger's. She might be able to handle college next year, "but she will need lots of support. Plenty of structure." However, she would never be able to work with people. So much for her dreams of becoming a teacher.

Alicia was devastated. Dr. Majithia, seeing the look in her eyes, tried to comfort her, saying, "This is not a life sentence." But to Alicia, that is exactly what it was! For so long she had fought so hard to overcome one neurological problem – OCD. She had come to Dr. Majithia's office to learn how she could continue to do so. Instead, she was told that she had yet another neurological condition – one that she could never escape. Worse, Dr. Majithia had made the decision she had based largely on what her dad had said about her – which meant that he must also see her as a hopeless failure. Maybe that's all she really was.

> *It's never easy to find out that you have a disability. It may be especially hard during adolescence. It will take Alicia a long time to find her place in the world and to figure out what having Asperger's really means to her. In the meantime, she could really use some reassurance from a friend. Fortunately, a friend is waiting for her.*

The Clouds Are Big With Mercy

The next morning Alicia returned to school. As she entered the classroom, she saw Rhys across the room. He looked up and in a second was bouncing over to her. "Here it comes," thought Alicia, dejectedly. "That girl will have told him everything. He knows. He'll never see me as normal again. Pity and charity will replace friendship."

"Alicia, I missed you yesterday. When you weren't here, I really missed you." Surprised, she looked into his eyes. Not a shadow of pity, charity, or even concern. His eyes held nothing but delight.

In that moment, Alicia didn't care how Dr. Majithia saw her or even how her father saw her. And through the years to come, whenever that appointment came back to haunt her, she remembered Rhys' eyes, and she tried to see what he saw.

She and Rhys never talked about the appointment or about Alicia's mental health. They just went on as before. But Alicia had learned something important about Rhys. It didn't matter whether he knew or didn't know about her illness. To him, she would always be Alicia.

© Copyright 2006
Alicia Adams
40 Peony Ave Apt. 14
Middletown PA 17057

Chapter Ten: The College

The diagnosis of Asperger's syndrome was made about seven months before Alicia left home for college. A lot could have been done in those seven months to help her understand her disability, and to prepare her for the challenges that lay ahead. She could have been taught to understand her specific needs and to advocate for herself when necessary. Her chosen college could have been informed of her disability and a support system created: a counselor could have even been prepared to take over where Mr. Havrilla left off. Such intelligent planning can make all the difference to a young person with obsessive compulsive disorder, Asperger's syndrome, or learning disabilities.

None of these things happened in Alicia's case. Her parents did not accept the diagnosis of Asperger's, and so the matter was simply dropped. Not that they were convinced of Alicia's readiness for college, but they did not believe that Dr. Majithia had any answers worth pursuing, and they made no attempt to find someone else who did. Mr. Havrilla wrote the admissions department at GMB to explain her diagnosis of OCD and possible need of continued counseling, but simply left out the likelihood of her also having Asperger's. The college never replied to his letter. Some time later Alicia was accepted as a student, yet her mental illness was never again mentioned. No attempt was made to create a support system for this very vulnerable teenager.

Mr. and Mrs. Adams were worried, but assumed that nothing could really be done to help Alicia, so nothing need even be attempted.

The college she had chosen was hundreds of miles from home and from her doctor and counselor, and no supports had been created. She would be left to sink or swim, and she was very much afraid that she would indeed sink. Dr. Majithia had certainly not been optimistic and neither were her parents. All sorts of horrible possibilities filled her mind: having a relapse into clinical depression as soon as she arrived, failing courses because she couldn't concentrate, having to drop out of college within the first semester due to mental illness, perhaps even needing to be hospitalized because her illness was worse than ever before. Any or all of these things could happen; no one was more aware of that fact than Alicia.

Mr. Adams had come up with a possible alternative to GMB: Alicia could remain at home and take classes at the local community college. The idea did not appeal to her. For one thing, she did not particularly want to go on living at home; constantly having to worry about her parents' reactions toward her disease was taking its toll upon her spirit, and she felt that some distance between them would be healthy for all. More importantly, she had a real sense of "now or never;" it seemed imperative that she find out as soon as possible if she had the ability to succeed on her own. An older person would have considered other possibilities; but at eighteen, Alicia was still young enough to actually believe that her entire future hung upon her first few months of college. She had fixed upon GMB as being the place where she would learn to teach – and for that she was willing to risk a great deal.

All this was in her mind throughout that spring and summer. It was a time of anxious waiting – waiting for the events of the fall to decide her fate. Was she doomed to failure, as the doctor and her parents seemed to think? In her mind, everything else seemed trifling in comparison to that question, and there was no shortcut to the answer. She could think of nothing to do but wait and hope for the best.

None of Alicia's anxieties were apparent to her friends at school. In many ways, she was happier and more confident than ever before; she appeared to be just as carefree as the rest of her class. It wasn't an act: while she was with them, especially with Rhys, she could forget for awhile that a giant question mark hung over her head. She could get caught up in the joy of the moment, like any other high school senior. The fears for the future returned only when she was alone: when she was wondering just how sick she would get in her first weeks of college and whether she had any chance of passing for normal.

The present and the future were such distinct entities in her mind that it never occurred to her to wonder what would happen to her new-found friendships after graduation, which was approaching rapidly. She never made plans to keep in contact with any of her friends, for she could not imagine losing them - she had never before had friends to lose.

Towards the end of May, Alicia caught yet another cold and as usual experienced a resurgence of her intrusive thoughts. She was exhausted, drained, yet determined to go on her senior class trip like everyone else. Although it was unusual for Alicia's colds to warrant medical attention, Mrs. Adams thought it worth consulting with the family doctor, who did not prescribe anything for the cold but was able to identify the real reason why Alicia's OCD got worse each time she became sick. The decongestants in her cough medicine were interfering with the Prozac. If Alicia had not been so tired, she would have been furious that she had suffered over *two years' worth* of unexplained relapses before anyone bothered to inform her of possible drug interactions. As it was, she was just glad to know that changing her cough medicine could prevent such relapses in the future.

She did enjoy the senior trip, in spite of her illness. It still had not sunk in that she and her friends would soon go their separate ways, not for a summer, but for a lifetime. Perhaps she was not alone in her obliviousness. Many of her classmates had been going to school together since kindergarten or at least elementary school; it was truly difficult to envision any other kind of life. And the last weeks of the school year went by so quickly! Graduation was all a blur. The main thing Alicia remembered afterwards was that her cap would not stay on, despite her friends' best efforts to affix it to her hair, and she had to carry it throughout the ceremony – while Rhys had troubles of his own, tripping over a graduation gown too long for him. It is passing strange how such trivial things can take up one's attention at important moments. It wasn't until later that Alicia realized that they hadn't even said goodbye.

For even after graduation, she still could not quite grasp the fact that she might never again see the people that had cheered and encouraged her all year. As yet she was not so much consciously missing them (she had never had much contact with her friends during the summers and did not expect it) as she was feeling the effects of being thrown on her own resources.

She had never consciously realized how much she'd grown to depend on Rhys to charm away her depression and anxiety (even if only for a few hours), and she did not fully realize it even now. His absence was more felt than acknowledged; she did not yet "miss" him in the usual sense. With no one to distract her from her anxieties, they became overwhelming. The intrusive thoughts re-emerged, not because of a drug interaction this time but because of her stress level. Yet Alicia masked her pain carefully. With all the pride and foolishness of youth, she didn't want her parents to know that just the prospect of going away to college was enough to make her sick. How would they ever trust her to handle the reality? She must show herself to be strong enough to face the ordeal that lay ahead.

It was to be a bigger ordeal than she could have possibly imagined. In Alicia's first weeks at GMB, she was tormented by the intrusive thoughts almost continually. She was prepared for that possibility, but what she was not prepared for were her roommates' attitudes. In high school, it had been a matter of course for Alicia to ask for prayer for her "neurological problem." Although she seldom went into detail about the illness, most of her classmates were more or less aware of her daily struggles and they had respected her for the way she handled her own personal crisis. It was only Rhys that Alicia had felt a need to hide her OCD from – and only so that he would not pity her. So Alicia saw no reason why she should not inform her roommates of her condition; she reasoned that it was better to bring up the subject herself than to have them stumble across her medicine bottle and wonder why she had a three-month supply of Prozac.

She would regret it. All three of her roommates – Amy, Lisa, and Rachel – had grown up in the same ultra-conservative Christian culture that GMB represented. Like the vast majority of GMB students, they had been taught that there was no such thing as mental illnesses, that all depression is the result of sin, that psychology is anti-Christian and utterly worthless, and that to seek psychological help is to deny the sufficiency of Christ.

Lisa was the worst. She was a nursing major, taking a course called Psychiatric Nursing. Actually, she was being taught every **lie** ever conceived about the mentally ill: that their illnesses were a fraud, their true problems either sin or demon possession, and their search for medical help an obvious lack of faith in God. In the first month they were roommates, Alicia was told repeatedly that if she were truly right with God, all her mental health issues would just disappear. She was told that the "happy pill" was nothing but a crutch. She was told that the doctors who had treated her were not to be trusted.

Alicia was not prepared to deal with any of this. She knew what Lisa and the other girls were telling her was wrong, but sometimes the only response she could make was an emphatic "No!" She knew she wasn't "helping her case" by becoming defensive, but she could not reason calmly with those who would undermine her fragile grip on health and sanity, and tempt her to forget all that she had so painfully learned about how to deal with her illness. Indeed, if she had thought anyone would understand, she might have replied, "Get thee behind me Satan." The matter was that serious: Alicia was, in a sense, fighting for her very life.

Readers may remember from chapter four that all too many Christians deny the existence of mental illnesses. As discussed earlier, Christians who are not reality-based make a false dichotomy between general revelation (truth discovered through observation and reason) and special revelation (truth from the Bible). All too many people have been conditioned to regard general revelation as being "secular" and ungodly. While such people are forced to accept general revelation in certain areas of life in order to function, they reject it in others. Generally, this leads to an artificial division of the person into a "spiritual" part (mind/soul) and a "physical" part (body and brain). Mental illness upsets such tidy categorization, and is therefore philosophically unacceptable.

Whenever Christian fantasy is protected at the expense of reality, slander is almost inevitable. Harsh attacks on the characters of both those who suffer from mental illness and those who treat it are delivered without hesitation, and without supporting evidence. Generally, such attacks make no distinction between psychological theories such as those of Freud or Jung, and observable facts about specific mental illnesses (even illnesses that have been proven to have a biological origin); nor is a distinction made between scientific research that has been rigorously reviewed and the pop psychology of self-help books or talk radio.

The fruits of such muddled thinking are poison to the mentally ill, and Alicia is right be on the defensive against it. She is right to reject an ideology that, quite simply, would kill her. But she is young and it is hard for her to do so. It was hard enough for her to suffer from a frightening disease, but now she must also bear the condemnation of those who would deny the reality of her suffering. She is not alone; many have been hurt far more by the prejudices of others. Discouraged from seeking proper medical help, too many seriously ill people suffer for years from illnesses that could have been successfully treated in a few weeks or months with a reality-based approach.

> *It is tragic when people suffer this way; it would be tragic if it were out of mere ignorance. But the phenomenon actually runs deeper than that. Why is there such an antipathy to psychology in many churches? The character of one of Alicia's roommates, Lisa, may hold a clue.*

Alicia was not so naïve that she didn't realize there was a possibility that her roommates would not be aware of the reality of mental illnesses. She herself had grown up in a cultural framework similar to theirs and before she became ill with OCD, she had accepted certain prejudices without much thought. It had been hard for her, in the early days, to refrain from spiritualizing her illness; not just because the intrusive thoughts dealt with "spiritual" matters, but because she had absorbed the all-too common assumption that real Christians don't get depressed, or if they do, then surely they will gain victory over it through their faith in Christ. It had been a long slow process for her to understand that "victory" over pain and sorrow is not something we are promised on this earth, and that the Christian life has a lot to do with endurance of the sorrows of this world – not the avoidance of them.

So she was to a certain extent prepared to educate her roommates. However, things didn't quite work out the way she expected. Even though Alicia "knew better," she knew beyond any reasonable doubt that her doctors had not lied to her and that her illness was a biological reality, she was still unexpectedly intimidated by Lisa's attitude. Although what Lisa said was blatantly untrue; Alicia was shaken by the confidence with which she said it and the fact that she had no concern at all for the pain she was inflicting on an already suffering fellow creature.

Lisa rather enjoyed inflicting pain, actually. She was a strong proponent of what she called "tough love" and what might more accurately have been described as "bullying." She had a personal contempt for "weak" people: those who admitted to having problems, those who were willing to admit that they were depressed or anxious.

An odd trait for a nurse, maybe, but her desire to go into the nursing profession had little to do with helping people and a lot to do with proving that she was stronger than they were.

Like many students at GMB, Lisa had been a victim of physical abuse throughout her childhood, at the hands of very religious parents who given her an astonishingly warped idea of what love is. She did not understand tenderness or mercy, having never experienced either. She could not even be kind to herself: she had been anorexic for several years, and had just recently begun to eat normally again. She prided herself on her will-power in overcoming anorexia without any help from anyone; she used that fact as "proof" that psychological help was unnecessary. Yet even Alicia, as young and naïve as she was, soon realized that Lisa was far from well: she would frequently exercise to the point where she would turn faint or even pass out, and defended her abuse of her body with the slogan, "pain is weakness leaving the body," which is medically nonsense. Her bullying of others and of herself stemmed from the same root: the abuse in her past that she was unwilling to deal with.

There were many Lisas at GMB, among both students and administration.

There are certain churches and colleges which attract an unusually high percentage of people from abusive or dysfunctional backgrounds. They are not, as one would hope, the more compassionate or reality-based institutions. All too frequently, the most damaged and needy people are drawn to churches or colleges in which they can best maintain the illusion that they are not really damaged at all. They are driven to "normalize" their past experiences, even when their home life may have been very abnormal and harmful.

Alice Miller explains, "In order not to die, all mistreated children must totally repress the mistreatment, deprivation, and bewilderment they have undergone because otherwise the child's organism wouldn't be able to cope with the magnitude of the pain suffered. Only as adults do they have other possibilities for dealing with their feelings. If they don't make use of these possibilities, then what was once the life-saving function of repression can be transformed into a dangerous destructive and self-destructive force."

Miller is writing about the most extreme example of denied abuse, that of Nazi Germany. There are some eerie parallels between Nazi ideology and the less articulated beliefs of the "Lisas" Alicia encountered. There are predictable consequences to living in denial of the facts of one's existence. One such consequence is the likelihood of being drawn into groups of people who share similar experiences and a similar desire to believe that all is well. Although these groups may take radically different forms (political parties, cults, gangs, or colleges) and may differ very much in philosophy and practice, they share a similar function: they offer the appearance of security to some desperately insecure people.

Such groups share a similar method as well: by expressing contempt for the weak and hurt, members avoid dealing with their own feelings of weakness and pain. One thing Alicia was especially struck with in her first months at GMB was the frequency in which "jokes" were made about people with mental illnesses, or even more strangely, about people who had suffered abuse. These did not seem like joking matters to her. What was so funny about needing medication or counseling, about psychiatrists or support groups, or worst of all, about a young child being hurt or beaten? It took a very long time for her to understand that such jokes were told not to amuse others but to express contempt for people who were considered "weaker." Strength was a cardinal virtue at GMB. You could be ignorant, insensitive, or even pointlessly mean, and no one would reproach you for it – instead you would probably be respected, and very possibly given authority over students less well regarded than yourself.

But heaven help the student who dares admit to having a weakness: especially if the weakness is a mental illness.

© Copyright 2006
Alicia Adams
40 Peony Ave Apt. 14
Middletown PA 17057

Chapter Eleven: Trapped

One might think that those who deny mental illnesses would be opposed to all counseling, but that's not the case. In fact, they might do less damage if they were! Instead they promote a type of counseling that stresses confronting the counselee with the "truth" that his or her problems are caused by sin and can be cured through repentance. Counselors are warned not to allow the people they counsel to attribute their problems to illness and not to consider any non-spiritual causes. Alicia is about to discover firsthand what such an approach can be like.

After a month at GMB, Alicia stepped into the counselor's office. She had had more difficulty setting up this appointment than she expected. Nobody – not the dean or the counseling department – had ever seen the letter that Mr. Havrilla wrote detailing her need for counseling, the letter that had been the only attempt at ensuring that she would have the support system that she would need in college. That should perhaps have warned her that something was not right, but she felt certain that at last she was to speak to someone with medical training, someone who would know about OCD. Her roommates might be ignorant and prejudiced, but surely the whole college couldn't be!

What Alicia didn't realize was that the "training" Miss Hibbard had received had been deficient in some essential points. She had no background in psychology, certainly none in disorders such as OCD. On the contrary, she had been taught, like Alicia's roommates, that secular psychology had nothing to offer ("the wisdom of God is greater than the wisdom of man") and that mental health problems were really spiritual problems. Her role was to uncover the sin in their lives and direct them to God's forgiveness and healing. She and Alicia were to be like people speaking different languages.

"Do you have assurance of salvation?" she asked Alicia.

"Yes."

"Tell me about your devotional life."

"I read the Bible every evening, and pray quite a bit throughout the day."

"And do you listen to the teaching in chapel?"

"Yes," said Alicia, who was wondering what the purpose of this interrogation was. But perhaps it was just Miss Hibbard's way of getting to know a new counselee.

"And now, why are you here?"

Alicia explained that she was being treated for depression and obsessive-compulsive disorder. When Miss Hibbard didn't know what obsessive-compulsive disorder was, she attempted to embark on an explanation of the neurological basis of OCD. "There's an enzyme that I'm lacking that acts as a vacuum cleaner. You see, every thought leaves behind it a trail of neurotransmitters…"

"Don't tell me about the neurotransmitters," said Miss Hibbard, whose training had not included anything so technical. "Just tell me what actually happens."

"It's thoughts… coming into my head that I don't mean, that I didn't put there. They just slam into my head like bricks! The first one came into my head while I was praying even, just slammed right in. And they kept coming and made me sick."

The Clouds Are Big With Mercy

Miss Hibbard, trained to consider all problems as spiritual, formed the idea that Alicia was dealing with some kind of recurring temptation. The rest of the conversation would be shaped by this misconception.

After dismissing Alicia's diagnosis with an airy, "Psychologists make these things up because they like to have labels for everyone," Miss Hibbard went on to ask, "Have you acted on any of these thoughts?"

"No," said Alicia, who was confused by the question and didn't know what else to say. What in the world did Miss Hibbard mean by acting on the thoughts? There was no way one could have acted on thoughts like hers – they were all in the form of statements rather than directions!

"Praise God for that! Have you tried replacing the thoughts with Scripture?"

"That's not possible. You see, the thoughts go on even when I am thinking of something else…"

"I disagree. You can't have two different thoughts at the same time!"

"I can. It's like having the radio on all the time – you can think about other things, but you never stop hearing it."

Miss Hibbard was not one to let go of an idea, and the radio analogy made no sense to her. "You can't have two different thoughts at the same time. What you need to do is take a passage of Scripture, memorize it, and repeat it whenever the thoughts come to your mind. You can overcome them through the power of the Word."

Alicia sat silent. There were just so many things wrong with what this woman had said that she gave up all hope of ever being able to put her straight. And she had been told that this was a trained counselor, one who could help her.

Alicia would not ask anyone for help for another two years.

No one suffering from a mental illness should be treated the way Alicia was. This young girl, only eighteen years old, had already undergone years of suffering because

of her illness, bearing her burden as bravely and cheerfully as she could, only to be condemned for having a disease that was not supposed to exist. She trying to be responsible for herself by seeking out a trained counselor; she found that the only counselor available was ignorant and prejudiced.

Worse, the treatment recommended was actually harmful: the worst thing someone with OCD can do is try and replace the intrusive thoughts with something else, as Alicia had discovered earlier when a sympathetic yet ill-informed Bible teacher gave her the same advice. Remember, attempts to suppress the intrusive thoughts through compulsive behaviors are always counterproductive. As we learned in chapter one, people with OCD have a problem with the brain's processing center or filtering station, the caudate nucleus. When this processing/filtering center is functioning normally, shifting from one thought to the next is easy and natural; "extra" or misdirected thoughts are filtered out. When caudate nucleus becomes "stuck" and can not filter out the brain's "extra" thoughts, it is not possible to suppress them through an act of the will. Rather, with the increase of frantic messages to the already clogged processing/filtering center, the jam gets worse, anxiety rises, and the malfunctioning areas of the brain become more hyperactive and more "stuck."

Alicia doesn't know all the science involved, but after nearly three years of living with OCD she has thoroughly absorbed the most important fact about it: <u>compulsive behavior doesn't work, it only causes more problems</u>. It doesn't matter if the compulsions are mental or physical; or whether they are totally illogical or apparently rational and "spiritual." All compulsive behavior makes OCD worse. Because she knows this, she doesn't believe what Miss Hibbard says.

What would happen, however, if someone came to Miss Hibbard when he or she first developed the symptoms

> *of OCD? The possibility is almost too horrible to be contemplated, yet it is a reality for many people in very conservative churches or schools. Some have been driven to suicide by people like Miss Hibbard. It is a shame such counselors can not be charged with malpractice.*

The two years Alicia spent at GMB are indescribable. In theory, she was free to leave; yet in reality she was not. She was lied to, just like every other freshman in the school was lied to. The GMB administration knew that within a few weeks or months most of its freshmen students would be frustrated and depressed and would want to leave the school. They expected this and did nothing to improve the lot of the unfortunate students. But in order to prevent mass transfers to other colleges, which would have been as disastrous for the school as it would have been beneficial to the students, freshmen were regularly told that if they left (as many wished to do) they would be failures for the rest of their lives, that they would quit everything that got difficult, that they would wind up working in a gas station and mourning for all they had lost. One GMB official after another described, in detail, this horrible fate that, they declared, awaited all who left GMB.

A stable adult would have immediately seen this for what it was: a pathetic attempt to manipulate or brainwash people into remaining in a school that had so little to recommend it that very few people would have stayed there voluntarily. Not so the more vulnerable eighteen-year-old. Alicia, like many freshmen, was already terrified of failing, and already convinced that her entire life depended on this first year of college. The GMB administration knew this about college students, and uttered the most preposterous claims with complete confidence of their being swallowed hook, line, and sinker.

And so Alicia was trapped! Trapped in a world where she was forced to deny the reality of the illness that she suffered from every single day, forced to conceal her own beliefs when they differed in any particular from that of the college president, forced to hide the fact that she was miserable at GMB. For the administrators had come up with a way of dealing with that too: constantly telling the students that they ought to be happy at college and that it was entirely their own fault if they were not. As a result, the students became masters at hiding their true feelings and their real thoughts, lest they be expelled for complaining or arguing. Like citizens of a police state, or members of a cult, they lived in a constant state of anxiety – exactly what Alicia did not need.

Perhaps the most tragic thing about that period in Alicia's life was that she came to GMB very eager to be social and to make friends. That was never really true of her before she met Rhys.

Just by his attitude toward her, he had made her feel that she was a loveable person just the way she was, and so she went off to school wanting to find that kind of acceptance again. But at GMB the only way she could be accepted was to hide whatever made her different from other people.

She did make friends at GMB – she used the social skills she had learned in her last year of high school, and tried to be the funny, social person Rhys had shown her that she could be. She was not entirely unsuccessful – she soon discovered that people everywhere will appreciate someone who can make them laugh. On the surface she was doing very well socially: she was certainly far more outgoing and talkative than she had ever been before. She acted carefree and sociable. But there was a poison all through it because she could only affect openness; she dared not be genuinely open. There was so much that had to be suppressed all the time. After awhile she was even hiding her real thoughts and feelings from herself. She almost forgot what it was like to be genuinely happy; she almost believed the GMB administrators' claims that of course, all the students were happy to be there. The human mind is more open to suggestion that most of us dream possible.

Especially at eighteen years of age.

Alicia is a young, vulnerable college student who is living in a world of lies: lies about her mental illness, lies about the college itself, lies about the world outside, even lies about her own emotions. She is in fact being subjected to a form of brainwashing that has been successful with countless young people, many of them more stable than herself. She lives in a world where to speak the truth – if it contradicts the accepted lies – is dangerous because it can lead to expulsion, a fate she has been led to believe is almost equivalent with death. She lives in a world where she can't trust anyone, even those she lives with: they might report her to the authorities if she displeased them or if they felt they were obligated to report a dissident in their midst. How does one continue to live in an atmosphere so toxic to life?

The human mind, though vulnerable in so many ways, is also equipped with means of defending itself. In particular, our minds have a mechanism for dealing with ongoing pain, such as that Alicia experienced during her two years at GMB. The mind employs a type of anesthetic known as disassociation. "The original purpose of disassociation is to separate conscious awareness from some emotional pain we are experiencing, to dis-associate one from the other," Dr. Mate explains. Generally, people use disassociation when they are in severe distress and feel helpless to escape from it in any other way; they are most likely to use this coping mechanism when pain is ongoing and no relief is in sight.

In her early days at GMB, Alicia felt a great deal of frustration and anger, and she was fully conscious of it. She knew that what the college was doing to her was wrong, and she wanted out. But as time went on, that was no longer the case – not because things had gotten any better, but because she had been taught to suppress her true

> *feelings in favor of those that were "safe" to have, that she was "allowed" to have.*

At times it was as if she were being torn in two. She was determined not to allow "them" to get "into her head," – she would not surrender to groupthink. She would not be pressed into the mold, like countless other students had been; she would survive as a thinking person. Yet it was also necessary to survival that she avoid attracting any attention to herself. She must appear to be exactly like everybody else, although she was not. She grew increasingly secretive during those two years, as she became more and more aware of the level of conformity that was expected at GMB. Sometimes it felt like everything was real about her had to be kept a secret and at times she had a hard time even *remembering* what was real.

Sometimes she wondered if everybody around her was crazy or if *she* was; the whole world just seemed so dark. That's when she thought about Rhys. He had never answered the letter she wrote him in the first few weeks of freshmen year. Alicia had scarcely taken the time to wonder why. She was too preoccupied with her day-to-day survival for either the past or the future to seem entirely real. It seemed a lifetime since the day they had forgotten to say goodbye. Yet sometimes she could still almost hear his laughter – or see his eyes lit up with joy – and in that memory she would find some measure of strength, or at least a reason to take fresh hold of the strength she had already. She would not let GMB swallow up the girl that he had known. She would not leave disgraced or defeated. She would stay two years and then transfer to college that offered a special education major – just like she'd planned.

And so she did. She would not allow herself to forget what she had learned about her illness; in fact, during those two years she became more skilled at Re-labeling and Re-attributing than ever before. Now that it was unmistakably a question of survival, she declined to exchange her sanity for the delusions she had been offered by her roommates and by the counseling department.

Years later, she wrote:

> "I arrived at GMB to find that in my struggle with OCD I would have no support at all; that in fact I was better off hiding my illness altogether. No one I knew was capable of dealing with it, and few were even willing to acknowledge the reality of my disorder. I had to live with the danger that I could grow worse and that no one around me would be able to help; thankfully, that did not happen. Those years were frustrating and lonely; even now it can be painful to remember them.
>
> But in the darkness of those days, God's grace shone brighter than ever before. He was my support; I had no other. I clung to the promise of 2 Corinthians 12: 7-10. Like Paul, I had a thorn in my flesh, and I pleaded with God to take it away – not just three times but more like three thousand. I wanted to be healed more than anything in the world, not just because of the pain of the disorder itself, but because those around me kept sending the message (sometimes blatantly, sometimes subtly) that I shouldn't have it: that a Christian shouldn't have a mental disorder, shouldn't need Prozac, shouldn't have to see a psychiatrist twice a year. I thought that instant healing would not only be more pleasant for me but also more "spiritual" than the long battle.
>
> Like Paul, I found that God thought otherwise. He didn't heal me when I was at GMB. In some ways my condition didn't change at all during those two years. "But he said to me, 'My grace is sufficient for you, for my power is made perfect in weakness.' Therefore I will boast all the more gladly about my weaknesses, so that Christ's power may rest upon me." Christ's power

truly rested upon me; He did not remove my weakness or make it irrelevant, but He used it to bring glory to Himself in ways I don't fully understand. He enabled me to remember what I had learned about managing my disorder and to practice it faithfully – something I hadn't previously been able to do without the support of a human counselor. Every day, I took my medication, tried my best to avoid compulsive behavior, and refused to give in either to the thoughts or to the misconceptions of those around me. The obsessions remained, but I became much better at coping with them. "

She wrote this to the administration of GMB, as part of an appeal on behalf of its current students. Nothing can change what happened to her at that school, but it was her prayer that by speaking truth to power she might improve the lot of others with mental illness.

She is still waiting for a reply.

© Copyright 2006
Alicia Adams
40 Peony Ave Apt. 14
Middletown PA 17057

Chapter Twelve: Hope

Six years had passed since Alicia's first experience with the intrusive thoughts. In those six years, she had never been free from them for more than eight months at a time, and perhaps two years altogether. She'd been through three clinical depressions by the time she was seventeen. She had waited until her senior year of high school to make friends, and then lost them upon graduation. For the last two years she had been a virtual prisoner of a cult-like institution. She was now twenty years old, and headed toward a college she had not yet seen. Her hopes were not too high. For all she knew, her new school, Buttonwood University, might not be much different from the last.

But it was as different as night and day. She could sense that from her first few days there – indeed, almost from the first few hours. She was so used to living in an atmosphere of repression and tension that its absence was startling. Far more startling than putting on a new pair of glasses and discovering how much clearer the world can be – it was almost like learning how to breathe again. It was a continual surprise to Alicia, that first quarter, to see just how comfortable and relaxed the students were, and how welcoming to a stranger. The climate of suspicion was entirely absent. There were no spies to ensure that Buttonwood students followed the rules; there weren't even that many rules. Certainly no one was anxious about being denounced as "not conforming to the spirit of the college" and expelled. Strangest of all, there was no fear of the administration or faculty; many people actually had an unfeigned respect and affection for those that taught and led them. In short, the girls she met were actually, unmistakably, genuinely HAPPY!

The culture shock was incredible. In those first two weeks at Buttonwood, Alicia was daily and almost hourly stunned by the freedom and the warmth of all she met. The change was welcome, but overpowering, especially when combined with the more usual stresses of transferring to a new school halfway through one's college experience. It came as a further surprise to her that her roommate Jane and their next-door neighbor Ann anticipated and sympathized with the difficulties she was experiencing, offering unsolicited encouragement as she tried to adjust to a completely different world.

Their support was more needed than they knew. While at GMB, Alicia had been under constant pressure, but it was a predictable pressure. She had learned to operate in a survival mode, and in fact had done so for so long that she had forgotten that there was another kind of life. Coming to Buttonwood gave her a chance of living differently, which was wonderful and yet terrifying. In a way, it was like the feeling she had had during her first weeks on Prozac, so long ago now. She felt that the cage door was open and yet she could not yet come out.

Paradoxically, her OCD symptoms had worsened by her second week at Buttonwood. The thoughts, which she had so long managed by constant Re-labeling and Re-attributing, were manageable no longer. She wasn't sleeping and had begun vomiting from stress, something she had hardly ever done at GMB. She had that strange time warp sensation that she had experienced at sixteen, when her medication was stopped too soon. The four years in between seemed like a dream – if an astonishingly long and detailed dream – and Alicia had the oddest sense of having been carried back to where she was when she first relapsed back into OCD. The intrusive thoughts were the same as they had been for the past four years, yet strangely enough she was feeling as overpowered by them as if she were once again sixteen years old. Was this the breakdown she had feared when she first went to college?

If so, it was short-lived. Alicia might feel that she had gone backward, but she did not forget what she had learned about Re-labeling and

Re-attributing. Most remarkable of all, she was brave enough to seek out help for the first time in two years. She confided her struggles to Ann and then to Jane, and was delighted to learn that, while they might not know very much about OCD, were willing to learn and respectful of what she had gone through. They prayed for her and with her, asked her what they could do to help, and told her often that they were glad that she had come to Buttonwood. Ann in particular was eager to reassure her that "None of us have it all together," and encouraged Alicia to talk more, and to talk more openly, than she was accustomed to do. Much to her amazement, she found herself telling Ann and Jane not only about her struggles with OCD, but also about some of her difficult experiences at GMB. The girls were shocked to learn of the conditions that students like them were being subjected to. After two years of not being allowed to complain, ever, Alicia found it very gratifying to finally tell the truth about GMB – and she was delighted at her new friends' interest.

Ann and Jane, through their compassion and genuine interest in their new friend, got Alicia through those first hard weeks, and would scarcely even allow her to thank them for their kindness. "That's what friends are for," Jane said. At last Alicia had to come to a point where she could accept their friendship with no fears that they were somehow using her. The seeds of self-doubt and mistrust that her teacher had planted so many years ago were almost entirely uprooted now. Knowing Rhys had been the beginning of a great change in her life. She had continued to develop socially while at GMB. In the supportive atmosphere of Buttonwood, she was to blossom into a much more confident young lady and a loving friend to many of the girls she met – starting with Ann and Jane.

There was so much baggage for her to work through that first quarter at Buttonwood. Remembering Miss Hibbard, Alicia was fearful about trying counseling again, but with Ann and Jane's encouragement, she consented to give it a try. The contrast could not be greater. Sally, the counselor, was very much like Ann and Jane in her attitude toward Alicia – warm and supportive, eager to encourage rather than to find fault. While she didn't have any specific training in OCD either, she was open to learning about it and allowed Alicia to explain her own disorder and how she'd learned to deal with it. Sally could offer little but encouragement to keep up the good work, but at this point in her life Alicia didn't really need that much help to deal with the intrusive thoughts. Just one month into her time at Buttonwood, they were already fading away, and would soon be gone completely.

It was about this time that Jane returned to the dorm room one evening to find Alicia dancing about with a bottle of water. "I'm thirsty! I'm thirsty!" Alicia cried, delighted. Jane eyed her admittedly mentally ill roommate with confusion and perhaps alarm. Alicia hastened to explain that a dry mouth was a side effect of Prozac, and its reoccurrence meant that the medication was once again "kicking in" after being temporarily undermined by the stress of a new place. Jane was happy for her friend – and perhaps relieved that said friend had not gone completely unhinged!

On the contrary, Alicia was taking hold of life – especially as the weeks passed and it became evident that this was no temporary decrease of the intrusive thoughts, but a complete recovery, rather like that she had experienced at age fifteen when she first started taking Prozac.

At first it seemed strange to her to be without the thoughts, because so much of her life for the past four years had been about managing them. She had become resigned to her life with OCD, and now she had to adjust to a life without OCD symptoms. It was a dramatic shift in mindset, but it was achieved surprisingly quickly, as her interest in all that Buttonwood had to offer encouraged her to look outward rather than remain trapped within her own head. Her changing outlook was reflected in her counseling appointments as the focus shifted from the OCD itself to its impact on her relationships with her parents, and then to the difficulties she'd had with making friends and how they were now being overcome. In a remarkably short time, there seemed to be no need for continued counseling, and Alicia and Sally parted as friends.

As Alicia flung herself into her new life as a Buttonwood student, reveling in new friends and new freedoms, she at times had an odd experience of "reliving her past" and having a chance to correct some of the things that had gone wrong for her before. When she first came to

Buttonwood and became suddenly ill with the resurgence of intrusive thoughts, she had that "time warp" feeling of being sixteen again and experiencing that significant relapse – only instead of being rejected and condemned for it, she instead experienced the compassion of understanding friends, and instead of the relapse being the beginning of a four-year battle, it was over in a few weeks. Alicia became aware, for the first time, how much of her life had been eaten away by the OCD. She wanted to make up for the lost time.

As she got better and was enjoying her new friends, she found herself remembering her very first friend, Rhys. She was thinking about him more than she had done in the past, and at last she let herself realize just how much he had really meant to her, and how much he still meant to her after all these years. For so long, her feelings for him had had to be pushed aside while she dealt with her day-to-day battle of OCD and surviving GMB. Now she was no longer operating in survival mode all the memories came crowding back: memories as fresh as if they'd parted only a few weeks earlier, and yet somehow sweeter for having been preserved so long.

As she began to understand what a difference knowing Rhys had made in her life, she longed to be able to thank him for all that he had done for her, all that she hadn't really acknowledged at the time. She wanted him to know that she remembered him and wasn't going to forget. Most of all, she wanted to see him again. It had been well over two years, but she could still hear his laughter and see the light in his eyes when he looked at her. Could it be possible that he remembered her too, and that their friendship could be renewed?

There was only one way to find out: she wrote to him – cautiously, for she was not about to say much about the hopes that stirred her heart. To her delight, he answered, explaining that he had never received her earlier letter and was glad to hear from her now. Their correspondence continued, off and on, for over a year. They sometimes talked on the phone, and once, over the summer break, they met at a small diner and talked for three hours – hours that Alicia considered among the happiest of her life.

But the years had changed Rhys in a way Alicia would never have dreamed of. She had not known that prior to transferring to their small Christian school Rhys had been known as a rebellious teen, frequently in trouble at school and at home. "Senior year was my shining moment," he explained to her. He'd not changed much at home, but before his school friends, Alicia included, he'd appeared as the good Christian boy. After graduation, however, he'd lost contact with all those friends, and fallen in with a quite different set of people. The life he'd been living since then was something Alicia very likely would not have understood even if Rhys had been willing to explain it to her.

He was, however, very cautious in what he told her. He did not actually lie to her, but he shied away from direct questions, giving only the vaguest of information. Alicia was hesitant to press him: she did not wish to offend, and at times she was frightened of what he might tell her. He might have realized that; he was far more aware than she was of the differences between them. Alicia was so naïve that she could scarcely take in what Rhys told her of his past and present life. She was convinced that the Rhys she had known and loved – that she still loved – was still in there somewhere.

It was for that Rhys that she prayed constantly, and to that Rhys that she wrote to with such confidence. He treasured her letters, saving them all and reading each one at least twice: the letters of a happy, innocent schoolgirl, enjoying her friends and her studies, eagerly anticipating a career as a teacher, and wanting so much to share her happiness with him. Yet he often failed to answer for weeks or even months at a time, and then suddenly began writing to her again. His charming and often humorous apologies ("I've been too busy to eat, sleep, or shower... not really, but pretty close!") offered no real explanation. Alicia was at a loss to understand this, until speaking with his mother in attempt to call him. The wise woman summed up the situation in a few words: "You represent what's good to him, Alicia, and that's what he's running away from." Alicia didn't know whether to be flattered or furious. She had never intended to "represent" anything but herself, and she could see no reason why Rhys' mysterious struggles should interfere with their friendship.

Meanwhile, her time at Buttonwood was passing quickly. Alicia was twenty-two years old and a senior. She had more friends than she could have dreamed of when she arrived. Some of her friends knew a little about her past experiences with OCD, but most of them did not. She had not experienced any symptoms of OCD since her first month at Buttonwood, a year and a half ago now. By the year after her "second recovery" from OCD, she was finding that it was increasingly difficult to remember to take her medication when she felt so well and so "normal." Yet her psychiatrist, who only saw her twice a year and knew little about the astonishing changes in her life, was not encouraging her to go off the medication yet, or indeed to consider going off it all – at least when she was in college. He explained that he often saw patients go off their medication and initially appear to be all right, but after three to six months, their initial symptoms would resurface, especially if they were under stress. "College is stressful," he insisted. "Wait until afterwards, if you really want to try going of the medication. But really it would be no problem if you were on it for the rest of your life."

Alicia thought otherwise. With a confidence that she could not have imagined as a GMB student, she began weaning herself off Prozac anyway, gradually cutting down from every day to every other day then to fewer and fewer times per week. She was alert for any possible changes in her thoughts or mood, but the only change that she noticed was an increase in her energy level – something that was very welcome as she was now entering her final year of college, working harder than ever, and loving every day of it. She was excited about her future as a special education teacher and eager to actually begin her life's work. It certainly seemed that all the troubles of her past were over. Her hopes were so high!

Later Alicia wrote of this period in her life:

> "I had such big dreams. It seemed like everything was going to go my way. I was getting off my meds. I had made it through the first block of methods courses and had every expectation of becoming a teacher. I had

seen Rhys again after four long years. And secretly I cherished another dream – I thought that my getting well again would somehow make my parents respect me, that we would be able to make a fresh start after all those hard years. I had heard so much from my Buttonwood friends about their good relationships with their parents, and I wanted that for myself. More than that, I had myself convinced that the only reason my parents and I didn't have such a good relationship was because I had OCD, and that everything was going to change once I was fully well."

She was about to find out that some things do not change, even when a mental illness is overcome.

© Copyright 2006
Alicia Adams
40 Peony Ave Apt. 14
Middletown PA 17057

Chapter Thirteen:
The Dreams Die, A New Life Begins

Years later, whenever Alicia remembered the September of her final year of college, the first thing she thought of was sunshine. Bright yellow sunshine, blue skies, and perfect weather – as if summer was never going to end. Alicia's interior weather or mood was brighter still. Classes were going well, she had more friends then ever before, and Rhys was writing to her about once a week, sometimes more. She finished weaning herself off Prozac with no problems. Life was just about perfect.

By October, however, things were starting to unravel. Alicia's practice teaching in a local elementary school was not going well. Although she did well with individual students or very small groups, her nonverbal learning disability made it difficult for her to be aware of the class as a whole. She "couldn't see the forest for the trees" nor could she attend to more than a few "trees" at a time. She would zero in on whichever students she was standing next to, while missing what was happening a few feet away. Unable to take in and respond to the massive amount of nonverbal information required to manage a classroom, Alicia was constantly frustrated as her carefully written lessons fell completely apart. The harder she worked, the worse things got. Her cooperating teacher tried to help, and so did her supervisor from the education department, but it was no use. Neither instruction nor example could give Alicia the nonverbal information processing that she lacked. By the end of the second week, there was simply no point in going on. With great sorrow, Alicia withdrew from that field experience.

It was heartbreaking. For the past six years she had dreamed of becoming a special education teacher. With that goal in mind, she had risked so much to go to college against medical advice. She had worked hard and come so close. It hurt to have to let that dream go. Alicia cried every waking moment for about twenty-four hours. She was still crying when she received an e-mail from Rhys, one of the first people she had told. He wrote:

> "I am so sorry that you are having difficulty on your career path. From the moment I heard that you were working with children, I knew that was for you. So I know that you are going to find another way to do what you want and love to do. There are programs for special needs kids that are one-on-one or very small groups; I'm sure your professors know more about that than I do. You are a very "personal" person; I think you were meant for that kind of setting anyways. And you know as well as I do that everything happens for a reason. Every cloud has a silver lining… hey, the sun just came out from behind the clouds as I was writing that…"

Alicia was still crying as she finished reading Rhys' words, but now she was smiling through her tears. Once again, her dearest friend had given her the gift of hope. She was still anxious and confused, but her mourning ended right there.

Within a few days, she and her advisor and the education department chair had come up with a plan that would allow her to graduate at the end of the semester with a degree in Special Education, although she would not have student taught and would not be eligible for teacher certification. She would be a very well-qualified teacher's aide. Alicia felt excited, although nervous, about graduating a semester earlier than expected and about starting a career that was rather different than the one she had planned on. She knew that she would miss her friends at

Buttonwood, and she wondered if she would really be able to get a job in the middle of the school year. However, she did like the idea of heading back to her home town and (she hoped) seeing Rhys more often.

Alicia intentionally put off telling her parents about the withdrawal from field experience and the subsequent changes in plans until she was able to discuss the matter perfectly calmly. (It took about three days.) She made a wise decision there. Her father meant to be sympathetic, but he lacked the capacity. It did not help Alicia to learn that her father was not surprised that she had failed – he had never believed that she would really be able to become a teacher. "Thanks a lot," she thought but did not say. It was not really a surprise to her that her parents' expectations of her were very low, but still it hurt to have that fact stated so bluntly. She ended that conversation as quickly as she could without being rude, and tried to forget it. Her father never knew that, once again, he'd hurt more than he'd helped.

For the remainder of that week Alicia basically "laid low." It was a much needed breathing spell, when the other students were completing their field experiences and Alicia was adjusting to the changes in her life. She knew that the Buttonwood grapevine would soon carry the news of her withdrawal from field experience to everyone she knew. She wasn't really ashamed of what had happened, but she wasn't all that eager to talk about it – although she cheerfully and bravely answered questions as the e-mails and phone calls began trickling in. She was comforted to find that everybody was very supportive and encouraging – at least after they got past the initial shock. Indeed, many of her friends were impressed with how well she was handling her disappointment, and admired her more, not less, than they had before.

The next week began the busiest period of her college experience – the final "block" of methods courses. For over a month, Alicia had little time for anything but schoolwork and certainly not much time to worry about her future. It was a happy time for her. Never before had she had so much energy and enthusiasm for her work. She was up early every morning and still working at midnight. Often, she'd take a few minutes to write to Rhys before shutting off the computer for the night – even though her roommate told her she was "spoiling that boy." Rhys was writing less often than before, but Alicia was not really concerned.

She was counting down the days until Thanksgiving, when she would see him again... and when she would be able to tell her parents that she had gone off Prozac and had no problems, even with the stress of withdrawing from field experience. The latter was a secret dream... one she scarcely dared to articulate, even to herself. The former... well, it occupied what time she had for daydreaming.

Fifty days to Thanksgiving... forty... thirty... twenty... ten... nine... eight... seven... six... five... four... three... two... one...

Yet when the longed-for holiday arrived, it was not as all as Alicia had envisioned. A few days before, she had caught a cold. It had been nearly two years since a cold had caused a recurrence of the intrusive thoughts, but this one did. Perhaps it was only to be expected, given the fact that Alicia was very "run down" and also that it was the first time she'd been sick since going off her medication. She wasn't actually alarmed. She had had enough experience with OCD to "feel" the difference between a temporary reoccurrence and a major relapse, and she knew this was the former. It was just that the timing was bad. Instead of being able to proudly announce that she was medication-free and doing fine, she arrived at home so obviously unwellthat her mother knew almost at once that Alicia was "low on Prozac" although she was surprised to learn that Alicia had not had any medication in over two months. Alicia had expected to be able to announce with pride that she was medication-free and doing fine, having beaten a very difficult disease. Instead she had to confess that she was once again suffering from a disorder that her parents had always resented. They regarded her with the mixture of concern and annoyance that was all too familiar. Alicia knew that the return of the intrusive thoughts was only a temporary setback, and that in another week she would once again be symptom-free, but she was angry about the poor timing. She felt that she'd been cheated out of the chance to prove herself to her parents. She hated having them know she was sick... and yet strangely enough she resented having to hide it from them. She felt that she'd been protecting them from the truth for too long already.

What was her father saying now? "Maybe it'll be all right. After all you've been stable for several years now. College seems to agree with you - Buttonwood and even GMB..."

At the mention of her old prison, Alicia's carefully constructed defenses broke down and without stopping to consider the consequnces, she burst out, "I was miserable at GMB! I had intrusive thoughts EVERY DAY I was there! I only stayed because I was too afraid too leave! I couldn't stand the thought of them beating me!" Hot, angry tears poured down her cheeks. She was a bit shocked at herself. She had long ago vowed to herself that her parents would never know the truth about GMB. In her more rational moods, she knew that they would never understand and that telling them would just make things worse. Yet just at this moment she was too flooded with emotion to hold her tongue.

Predictably, Mr. Adams was furious that Alicia had "lied" to him by not telling him about her suffering at GMB. Apparently he had forgotten all the times he had told her that he didn't want to know anything about what happened at school. "Ignorance is bliss," had always been his policy. Her first year at GMB, Alicia had been instructed to confine her letters to what she had eaten or whether she had done her laundry, on the grounds that anything else would only worry her mother. Alicia had almost forgotten how abandoned that had made her feel, as an already confused and lonely college freshman. She had tried not to think of it, and even pretended to herself that it had been her own idea not to tell her parents very much about her life. Now the old wound resurfaced. How could they have cut her off like that? And how could her father attack her now for doing what she'd been told?

Things were about to get much worse. For four long and difficult months, she had been waiting, no longing, to see Rhys again. She had no plans for what she would do or say when that golden moment arrived - all she could think about was seeing his dear face once more. But although Alicia waited with growing anxiety and was barely able to think of anything else, Rhys did not call nor answer her phone calls. By the Saturday after Thanksgiving, Alicia knew that he was never going to. She was angry and confused and heartbroken. She couldn't believe that Rhys would let her down now, after all those months of waiting. She knew that he had initially been very reluctant to see her again, but she thought that since they had talked this summer he had gotten over that. He had told her he'd call. She'd told him that she was looking forward to it. Yet after his assurances that she had only to let him know when she would be coming home, he could simply ignore her entirely. He hadn't had even the consideration to let her know or to make an excuse. She wanted to cry and scream and throw things all at once.

If Alicia had not been beside herself with grief, she would never have let her parents know that anything was wrong. She knew too well that they could not be trusted. But her rage against Rhys was too great to keep locked inside, and the same parents that had been so unprepared for the truth about Alicia's experiences at GMB were now forced to her about her disappointment in love. "This is the only thing - THE ONLY THING - I've been looking forward to all these months!" she screamed. That wasn't entirely true: she had also dreamed of a new relationship with her parents, but now both dreams mocked her with their impossibility. Was everything in her life destined to turn into a nightmare?

Mr. Adams took Alicia out for a drive that night... ostensibly to calm her down. Alicia should have known better than to ever get in that car. Her father had responded badly to every single crisis of her life, and exactly why he should do any better with this latest one is something Alicia herself could not have said. There's something deep inside the human heart that longs so much for empathy that it is willing to take incredible risks on the most remote chance of finding it. Maybe Alicia thought that ever her father could not remain completely untouched by a broken heart... that while he had been unable to handle her illness, he would surely do better when faced with a "normal" problem. If so, she was in for a very rude awakening.

Once they were alone Mr. Adams started screming at her, telling her what a fool she had been to believe that Rhys would ever be interested in her. He told her that he love for Rhys was nothing by a fantasy, a replacement for real friends. He kept saying how stupid she was and how selfish to upset the family with something that wasn't even real. Anyone else, even a complete stranger, would have known at a glance that Alicia's grief was very real indeed. All the time she was sobbing so hard that she could hardly breathe. She shook all over, though she didn't know whether it was from fright or cold. Her chest ached as if her heart was literally breaking within her. She had never known such raw pain, even in the midst of her depressions. Superimposed on all this grief over losing Rhys were horror and shock that her father could treat her so badly.

And yet... was it really so surprising? Alicia now recalled another drive through the rain, one that she had not allowed herself to remember in years: the time she had asked her father to take her home because her intrusive thoughts had given her a headache, only to have him rage against her for accusing him of giving her a headache. He treated her like garbage then and he was doing it again now. Why had she ever imagined that he would change? He had never shown the slightest sign of wanting to.

Alicia's heart was broken twice that night.

Family pathology is extremely complicated, far more complicated than any hurting adolescent wants to believe - and Alicia, for all her twenty-two years, is still an adolescent emotionally. Her OCD has consumed nearly five years of her life - important developmental years - leaving her with the maturity of a 17- or 18-year-old. Most teenagers have a "personal fable" that assures them that everything will be all right. Alicia's is the belief that all the problems she has had with her parents are because of her disease. This allows her to dream of a magically healed family. Her love for Rhys is not a fantasy, despite what her father may think, but her expectation of a better relationship with her parents certainly is. Her heartbreak over

Rhys will heal as the loss of a first love always does, but the loss of the dream of a healthy and loving family will prove to be a far more lasting trauma.

Alicia Adams

It would be long before Alicia could fully accept the fact that her family's problems were much deeper and more complicated than her OCD. Although she had been the "identified patient," her father was in many ways just as mentally ill and just as irrational as she ever was, and he had never sought help; he had been too busy trying to convince Alicia that she was the one with all the problems. For so long she had wanted to trust him so much that it was very difficult for her not to believe him, even when one painful experience after another showed that he would never be what she needed him to be. He was incapable of empathy and if he felt pressured to make an emotional response he would only attack her and humiliate her in any way possible. Her OCD did not make him that way and overcoming the OCD would not change him. It was a profound change for Alicia when she was finally able to stop blaming herself and her disease for everything that had gone wrong in her life. She wouldn't get there that Thanksgiving or even the next.

However, as all her girlish dreams were shattered, a new determination rose within her to make a new life for herself. It wouldn't be the life that she had dreamed of a few months before. She would never be a teacher, she'd never see Rhys again, and she'd never have the kind of father she felt she needed. She'd suffer a great deal, especially when she left the safe haven of Buttonwood and moved back home to live with her emotionally abusive father. There would be many days when she would want to die because her life seemed so hopeless, but still she'd find the courage to go on living and the patience to go on trying. Against all odds, she would build the life that she was meant to have.

© Copyright 2006
Alicia Adams
40 Peony Ave Apt. 14
Middletown PA 17057

Chapter Fourteen: Six Years Later

The classroom door opened and the camera man came in, peering through the lens of his video camera. He scanned the large, cherry room where four children were each engaged with their own instructor. The camera man tiptoed over to the nearest one.

Tiny Billy was at the play center, sitting on a soft Winnie-the-Pooh chair. Jan, a paraprofessional in this special education classroom, engaged him in play with various toddler-type toys. Billy did not seem to notice the presence of the camera man. His stubby finger jabbed at the music toy in his hand, and he flapped his arms with delight.

In the middle of the room, 7-year-old Beckett lay under a colorful quilt. Ran, another paraprofessional, lay next to him and tickled him and lightly pounded his chest. Beckett laughed hysterically, and gestured for still more of the physical play he loved.

Moving on to a work center, the camera man filmed Yancy, also 7 years old, as he worked with June, the speech therapist. June held up a photograph of a refrigerator. "What is it?" she asked. Yancy looked down at the laminated sheet in front of him, and pointed to the small icon of a refrigerator. "Bah!" he said.

June praised him and gave him a "token" - a spool or button backed with Velcro. Tokens are a valuable commodity in this classroom, as they can be exchanged for anything: favorite snacks, toys, or activities. Yancy added it to the four already attached with Velcro to the small plastic sheet he used as a token board, then scooped up his five tokens and handed them to June. He had been working for a beloved video cover that he had yet to tire of examining, but upon noticing the camera man he changed his mind. Leaping out of his seat he dashed over to the camera. He was not about to miss the chance to perform! He jumped up and down and blew kisses, clapping both hands to his forehead as the joy of the experience overwhelmed him. The camera man was delighted with his eager subject. He gave Yancy a minute or two of on-screen time, then let him look through the lens himself. Yancy squinted to look through the camera, but preferred being out in front. He followed the camera man on the next work center, still hopping up and down in delight.

Preston, almost nine, was holding the big green see-n'-say he had earned. He concentrated on it as if the fate of the world hung upon its song. "Our treehouse has the 26 letters a to z," it sang, as Preston spun its wheel. When his two minutes of reinforcement were up, Nadea, yet another paraprofessional, gave him the standard warning: "Three, two, one - treehouse is all done!" She quickly presented him with his choice board, a menu of small picture cards representing Preston's choices of rewards. Preston needed only a second to decide - he'd work for the treehouse again.

Nadea gave Preston a dry erase marker and a laminated sheet that displayed several lines and a circle. Preston's task was to trace and copy each one. He traced the figures easily but had difficulty copying. His lines ran right off the page. Nadea coached Preston through his assignment and rewarded any success with tokens. He "cashed in" and got the treehouse back just as the classroom timer sounded. It was time for the students to transition to their next activity. As the children moved toward their visual schedules, the camera man quietly left the room, chuckling as he thought of the little fellow performing for the camera. Those kids had been awfully cute.

These boys are just four of the amazing children that I, Alicia Adams, have had the privilege of working with over these past six years. I am now twenty-eight years old, and very different from the heartbroken adolescent whose dreams fell apart that fateful Thanksgiving. My work as a special education paraprofessional pulled me out of the depression and hopelessness that marked the first few months after college: through my work I found purpose, confidence, and the joy of using gifts I had not known I possessed.

At times, I have wondered if Rhys, somehow, had known. Certainly he had predicted my career path with remarkable accuracy; I have found my niche in delivering one-on-one, intensely personal services to children with severe autism. During that life-changing first year, with so many frustrations and triumphs, there were times when I wished that I could tell him how much his encouraging vision had meant to me at that very vulnerable time in my life. However, I never heard from him again. The letter I wrote to him after Thanksgiving, telling him how badly I'd been hurt by his failure to show up, may have had something to do with that, although he may have already decided not to continue the friendship. Perhaps Rhys felt that a clean break would be for the best. In time I came to adopt that view of it, realizing that Rhys had simply grown too far away from me, and that he could never again be the Rhys I had known and loved.

Healing from the relational struggles within my family was a far more complex matter. For years I had flashbacks about the cruel things my father had screamed at me over the years, and felt that I could never trust him again. I forgave him many times, only to become discouraged when hurt and anger rose up within me once more. I gradually came to feel that sometimes forgiveness was like overcoming OCD: a long battle with many setbacks and no clear victory, but one I must continue to fight. I thought it might be a lifelong battle, but to my surprise, our relationship became far less tense as I grew older and more realistic in my expectations of my father. As I no longer demanded more of him than he was able to give, he became less defensive towards me; as I proved that I was able to care for myself he became less anxious about me and less likely to express that anxiety in an antagonistic manner. In time, we came to understand each other better and our struggles were truly laid to rest.

For over four years, I did not have any significant reoccurrence of the intrusive thoughts that had plagued me in high school and college. Occasionally I felt the faint echoes of the thoughts, yet in a moment they were gone; only under great stress did they reappear for several days at a time, then vanished when I dealt with the problem situation. I knew that I was still vulnerable and that at some point I could possibly have a relapse, yet I relished the time of health and was determined to make the best possible use of it.

I considered whether it would be worthwhile to make a second attempt at becoming a teacher rather than a paraprofessional, and for a time took courses toward certification through a local university. However, I soon realized that the coursework was not remediating the problems that had kept me from being successful in my college field experiences. I decided to undergo neuropsychological testing to discover if I had a learning disability in the area of nonverbal processing, and if so, whether anything could be done about it. The answers were yes - I was officially diagnosed with nonverbal learning disability and/or Asperger's syndrome - and no, nothing could really be done about it.

I will never have the ability to oversee a busy classroom of children, paraprofessionals, and therapists. However, I have worked hard to develop nonverbal processing skills as much as my disability allows. Thanks to MapQuest (the perfect tool for someone who needs step-by-step directions) I seldom get lost while driving anymore, although I can still become disoriented in a new place. In an unfamiliar restaurant, I might walk into the kitchen while looking for the exit; in a strange movie theater I may be completely bewildered by the different hallways. I can laugh at mistakes like these, but difficulties in social situations are not so amusing. Through letters, e-mails, phone calls, and occasional visits I have maintained several of my college friendships and have no difficulty interacting with these familiar people. However, with anyone I have not known for years, I am still mostly hesitant and sometimes fearful.

Four years after I began her work as a special education paraprofessional, my greatest fear was realized: I had a relapse into OCD and depression. This time my intrusive thoughts and compulsive urges were accompanied by panic attacks and insomnia. Unable to sleep, unable to drive, unable to work, I found myself very dependent on my parents once more, a situation I had feared and hoped to avoid. Yet this time things were different. My parents were more informed and understanding than they had been ten years earlier. I was more self-controlled and less hysterical than I had been as a teen. As hard as that experience was, God used it to bring this sorely tried family back together. With the help of medication and counseling, and the support of my family and friends, I once again fought her way out of depression and became fully functioning again. Today, I am still on medication and expect to remain so for some time. I have been reminded of the fragility of mental health and emotional stability, and more appreciative of the life and health and peace she has been given.

I know that God can restore the years that the locust has eaten (Joel 2:25) and I eagerly looks for His miracles of restoration in her own life. Over and over again I have marveled at the amazing way God has led me through the wildernesses of mental illness, depression, emotional abuse, attempted brainwashing, and heartbreak. I've mourned for what I lost, given thanks for what I gained, and proved over and over that "God is good all the time, and all the time God is good."

My life is a testimony to that wonderful promise: "And we know that in all things God works for the good of those who love Him, who have been called according to His purpose." It's not because this story has a happy ending, although it does: I've grown into a happy, healthy, successful woman with OCD and Asperger's. However, long before any of these blessings came to be, my life demonstrated the grace of God because He lives in me. I would have been no less His child, and God would have been no less good, if I had not been healed.

The Christian poet William Cowper suffered throughout his life from a devastating mental illness that included OCD-like symptoms and multiple depressions, both quite untreatable in the 18th century. He never recovered; he made more than one attempt at suicide. Yet near the end of his sad life, he wrote this beautiful hymn that expresses much of what Alicia has experienced:

> *God moves in a mysterious way*
> *His wonders to perform;*
> *He plants His footsteps in the sea*
> *And rides upon the storm.*
> *Deep in unfathomable mines*
> *Of never failing skill*
> *He treasures up His bright designs*
> *And works His sovereign will.*
>
> *Ye fearful saints, fresh courage take;*
> *The clouds ye so much dread*
> *Are big with mercy and shall break*
> *With blessings on your head.*
>
> *Judge not the Lord by feeble sense,*
> *But trust Him for His grace;*
> *Behind a frowning providence*
> *He hides a smiling face.*
>
> *His purposes will ripen fast*
> *Unfolding every hour;*
> *The bud may have a bitter taste*
> *But sweet will be the flower.*
>
> *Blind unbelief is sure to err*
> *And scan His work in vain*
> *God is His own interpreter*
> *And He will make it plain.*

When I was fifteen I wanted nothing more than to get rid of the OCD at once and forget that I had ever had it. I could not have imagined what a very long journey it would be. Still less could I have imagined that I would one day be thankful that I was not healed instantly. For in my weakness, I learned to "trust in the Lord with all her heart, and lean not upon her own understanding." In my depression, I discovered the peace the passes understanding. As the college pressured me to believe its lies, I clung closer to the One who is Truth. In a time of heartbreak, I learned to say, "The Lord gives and the Lord takes away. Blessed be the name of the Lord." Hidden in those dark and frightening clouds were blessings I can't imagine life without. They were truly big with mercy.

Footnotes

1. http://www.autism.com/autism/index.htm

2. My battle with OCD and depression is chronicled in my first book, The Clouds Are Big With Mercy.
3. For detailed information about how services for autistic children (and adults) have evolved over the past few decades, read Unstrange Minds by Roy Richard Grinker.

4. http://www.autism.com/ari/editorials/ed_lettersupport.htm

www.ingramcontent.com/pod-product-compliance
Lightning Source LLC
Chambersburg PA
CBHW021112080526
44587CB00010B/487